Blake

Selected Poems

Edited by Mike Davis and Alan Pound

Series Editor: Andrew Whittle
Series Consultant: Virginia Graham

821·6 BLA

14215   108669   1 day

Heinemann Educational Publishers
Halley Court, Jordan Hill, Oxford OX2 8EJ
a division of Reed Educational & Professional Publishing Ltd

OXFORD   MELBOURNE   AUCKLAND
JOHANNESBURG   BLANTYRE   GABORONE
IBADAN   PORTSMOUTH (NH) USA   CHICAGO

First published 1996

06 05 04 03 02
10 9 8 7 6 5 4 3

ISBN 0 435 15082 0

Cover design by The Point
Text design by Roger Davies
Typeset by Books Unlimited (Nottm)
Printed and bound in the United Kingdom by Clays Ltd, St Ives plc

CONTENTS

Introduction

——————— Songs of Innocence ———————

——————— Songs of Experience ———————

The Marriage of Heaven and Hell

Other Poems and Extracts

Background

Critical Approaches

Select Bibliography

Index of First Lines

INTRODUCTION

William Blake (1757-1827), poet, artist and illustrator, was relatively un-
known in his own lifetime and his importance was only established later
in the nineteenth and twentieth centuries. Part of the reason for this was
the limited circulation of his works, most of which included hand-etched
and painted illustrations. An additional reason, however, was the per-
ception of him as 'mad', a myth which was perpetuated for many years
after his death.

More significantly, there is no doubt that Blake was at odds with his
age in many ways: artistically, politically and religiously. This was mani-
fest both in his radical ideas and in the unusual form taken by his artistic
and poetic expression. However, it was here that he made a major con-
tribution to the development in England of Romanticism – the intellec-
tual and artistic movement which grew up in opposition to the scientific
and rational philosophy of the eighteenth-century Enlightenment, and
which was associated politically with the revolutions in America and
France.

Blake's meanings do not always give themselves up easily and he was
aware of this himself. He wrote of his work: 'That which can be made
explicit to the idiot is not worth my care' (from a letter to the Revd. Dr
Trusler, 23rd August, 1799). However, he is very much in tune with late
twentieth-century sensibilities and has had a considerable impact on the
development of a counter-culture. This is because of his central appeal
to the emotions rather than the intellect and his celebration of freedom,
the imagination, the instincts. He rejected conventional values, which he
called 'the mind-forg'd manacles'.

This edition draws almost exclusively from the revolutionary *Songs
of Innocence and of Experience: Shewing the Two Contrary States of the
Human Soul* which constituted a break from earlier poetic forms and
introduced new themes. It also includes the whole of *The Marriage of
Heaven and Hell*. Apart from being interesting and demanding in its own
right this text, which is contemporaneous with *Songs of Innocence and
of Experience*, can be seen as Blake's intellectual and artistic manifesto.
Peter Ackroyd comments in his new biography of Blake that:

> It is the work of an angry, exalted young man who feels the truth of
> his own sexual and creative energies. It also displays his confidence

and ambition, because here for the first time he establishes himself in the role of artist-prophet. (Ackroyd, 1995: 153)

This edition also recognizes that a successful reading of Blake necessitates some understanding of the social and political context of his work and his place in the emergence of Romanticism. These matters are dealt with in discrete sections which provide a basis for further reading. The poems themselves are supported by short commentaries, glosses on difficult words and ideas and prompts to help interpretation and understanding. The Critical Approaches section takes this process further by exploring particular aspects of form and theme and the interrelationships that exist between the poems. It also includes relevant activities which lead towards formal essay questions of the kind students will find in 'A' Level examinations.

Mike Davis
University of Manchester

Alan Pound
University College of
St Martin, Lancaster

for Judy
for Vickie

Songs of Innocence

Introduction

Blake introduces the sequence with a poem about the creative process. A shepherd, piping to his sheep, has a vision of a child who inspires him to become a poet and compose the 'songs'.

5   *lamb* – capitalization in Blake's original version suggests that the reference is to Jesus.

8   *wept* – compare *Proverbs of Hell* in *The Marriage of Heaven and Hell*: 'Excess of sorrow laughs; excess of joy weeps' (page 97).

16   *reed* – used to make the 'rural pen'.

18   *stained* – as the paint on an artist's brush stains clear water.

20   *joy* – rejoice.

What are the stages which lead to the writing of the 'happy songs'?

Why do you think the child disappears?

Songs of Innocence

Introduction

Piping down the valleys wild,
Piping songs of pleasant glee,
On a cloud I saw a child
And he laughing said to me:

5 'Pipe a song about a lamb!'
So I piped with merry cheer;
'Piper, pipe that song again!'
So I piped – he wept to hear.

'Drop thy pipe, thy happy pipe
10 Sing thy songs of happy cheer!'
So I sung the same again
While he wept with joy to hear.

'Piper, sit thee down and write
In a book, that all may read.'
15 So he vanished from my sight
And I plucked a hollow reed.

And I made a rural pen,
And I stained the water clear,
And I wrote my happy songs
20 Every child may joy to hear.

The Shepherd

This poem continues the opening pastoral theme. Inevitably, Christian associations will spring to mind, e.g. Jesus as the Good Shepherd, but Blake may be concerned with the wider issue of good leadership.

1   *lot* – task or rôle.

2   *strays* – wanders.

8   *nigh* – near.

What does Blake see as the qualities of good leadership?

How does the poem suggest a wider delight in God's creation? You may like to consider features of language, rhythm and rhyme.

The Shepherd

How sweet is the shepherd's sweet lot!
From the morn to the evening he strays;
He shall follow his sheep all the day
And his tongue shall be filled with praise.

5   For he hears the lamb's innocent call,
And he hears the ewe's tender reply;
He is watchful while they are in peace,
For they know when their shepherd is nigh.

The Echoing Green

This is a simple – indeed idealistic – picture of earthly happiness which sees child/parent relationships and community life in terms of natural cycles.

9 *sports* – play in general.

13 *oak* – a symbol of security.

Why is the green described as 'echoing'?

What evidence can you find in the poem that Blake is aware of change and mortality?

The Echoing Green

The sun does arise
And make happy the skies;
The merry bells ring
To welcome the spring;
5　The skylark and thrush,
The birds of the bush,
Sing louder around
To the bells' cheerful sound,
While our sports shall be seen
10　On the echoing green.

Old John with white hair
Does laugh away care,
Sitting under the oak
Among the old folk.
15　They laugh at our play
And soon they all say,
'Such, such were the joys
When we all, girls and boys,
In our youth-time were seen
20　On the echoing green.'

Till the little ones weary
No more can be merry,
The sun does descend
And our sports have an end;
25　Round the laps of their mothers,
Many sisters and brothers
Like birds in their nest
Are ready for rest,
And sport no more seen
30　On the darkening green.

The Lamb

In this apparently very childish poem, the child's words nevertheless show his pure understanding of a creative and redemptive God. You should compare this poem with *The Tiger* in **Songs of Experience**: a very different manifestation of God.

4   *mead* – field.

13   *He is called by thy name* – God the creator made the lamb but he is also Jesus, the Lamb of God, who died on the cross to save mankind from sin.

16   *He became a little child* – i.e. at Christmas when God became man.

18   *We are called by his name* – when christened, a child is named 'in Jesus'.

What, if anything, saves this poem from the charge that it is embarrassingly naïve?

What evidence can you find in the poem of a delight in God's creation?

The Lamb

     Little lamb, who made thee?
     Dost thou know who made thee?
Gave thee life and bid thee feed
By the stream and o'er the mead;
5 Gave thee clothing of delight –
Softest clothing, woolly, bright;
Gave thee such a tender voice,
Making all the vales rejoice?
     Little lamb, who made thee?
10   Dost thou know who made thee?

     Little lamb, I'll tell thee,
     Little lamb, I'll tell thee;
He is called by thy name,
For he calls himself a lamb;
15 He is meek and he is mild,
He became a little child:
I a child and thou a lamb,
We are called by his name.
     Little lamb, God bless thee,
20   Little lamb, God bless thee.

The Little Black Boy

Slavery was not abolished in Britain's overseas possessions until 1834 (after Blake's death) but long before this there were moves to end it, which Blake supported. Notice that it is the black boy's innocent voice which we hear – a deliberately provocative manoeuvre by Blake.

1 *southern wild* – Africa.

4 *bereaved* – dispossessed or divested.

13 *space* – time.

16 *cloud* – the physical body (see also line 23).
    grove – i.e. of trees (also protective, like the dark skin).

20 *golden tent* – a shelter, but also the notion of protective care (derived from 'attention').

24 *joy* – rejoice.

What challenge does hearing the voice of the black boy offer to the reader's complacency?

How does the meaning of the word 'heat' change in the poem?

The Little Black Boy

My mother bore me in the southern wild,
And I am black, but O, my soul is white!
White as an angel is the English child,
But I am black, as if bereaved of light.

5 My mother taught me underneath a tree,
And sitting down before the heat of day,
She took me on her lap and kissed me,
And pointing to the east began to say,

'Look on the rising sun: there God does live,
10 And gives his light, and gives his heat away;
And flowers and trees and beasts and men receive
Comfort in morning, joy in the noon-day.

And we are put on earth a little space
That we may learn to bear the beams of love;
15 And these black bodies and this sunburnt face
Is but a cloud, and like a shady grove.

For when our souls have learned the heat to bear
The cloud will vanish; we shall hear his voice
Saying, "Come out from the grove, my love and care,
20 And round my golden tent like lambs rejoice!"'

Thus did my mother say, and kissed me;
And thus I say to little English boy,
When I from black and he from white cloud free,
And round the tent of God like lambs we joy:

25 I'll shade him from the heat, till he can bear
To lean in joy upon our Father's knee;
And then I'll stand and stroke his silver hair,
And be like him, and he will then love me.

The Blossom

Ostensibly a poem which seeks to show the innocence in God's creation. However, some commentators have seen the poem as being about sexuality, ideally natural and innocent but not without the potential for sorrow. Compare it with *The Sick Rose* in **Songs of Experience** which seems to be about the destructiveness of furtive and illicit passion.

1 *sparrow* – traditionally (and especially in nursery rhymes) a happy bird; it has also been identified as a phallic symbol.

7 *robin* – traditionally a tragic bird, and in nursery rhymes contrasted with the happy sparrow.

Taking the poem at face value, how does it demonstrate the innocence of God's creation?

What evidence is there which would support a sexual interpretation?

The Blossom

Merry merry sparrow
Under leaves so green!
A happy blossom
Sees you swift as arrow;
5 Seek your cradle narrow
Near my bosom.

Pretty pretty robin
Under leaves so green!
A happy blossom
10 Hears you sobbing, sobbing,
Pretty pretty robin,
Near my bosom.

The Chimney Sweeper

Another poem, like *The Little Black Boy*, in which we hear an innocent speaker's voice. Young boys were sold to master-sweeps to climb up inside the chimneys of large eighteenth-century houses to clear the soot. This was dangerous and disease-prone work and many died. Despite this, the poem appears to have an optimistic perspective, by contrast with the contrary poem in *Songs of Experience*.

2   *my father sold me* – literally; sweeps paid parents for boys on a sliding scale according to age and size.

3   *weep* – i.e. sweep, but meant to hint at the boy's suffering and his extreme youth; younger, smaller boys were in great demand.

5-6   *his head ... was shaved* – a routine practice to prevent the boys' hair from catching fire; note also the comparison with sheep-shearing and remember the child/ lamb association in *The Lamb*.

12   *coffins of black* – the chimneys/the unhappy lot of the sweepers/the blackened bodies of the chimney sweepers/ bodies as prisons of the spirit.

17   *bags* – i.e. of soot.

20   *want* – lack.

> *Why do you think Blake included this poem in* **Songs of Innocence?**

> *What is the effect of the platitudes that the boy offers Tom by way of comfort at the end? Is this Blake's view?*

The Chimney Sweeper

When my mother died I was very young,
And my father sold me while yet my tongue
Could scarcely cry 'weep weep weep weep!'
So your chimneys I sweep and in soot I sleep.

5   There's little Tom Dacre, who cried when his head,
That curled like a lamb's back, was shaved; so I said,
'Hush, Tom! Never mind it, for when your head's bare
You know that the soot cannot spoil your white hair.'

And so he was quiet, and that very night,
10 As Tom was a-sleeping, he had such a sight!
That thousands of sweepers – Dick, Joe, Ned and Jack –
Were all of them locked up in coffins of black,

And by came an angel who had a bright key,
And he opened the coffins and set them all free;
15 Then down a green plain leaping, laughing they run
And wash in a river, and shine in the sun.

Then naked and white, all their bags left behind,
They rise upon clouds, and sport in the wind;
And the angel told Tom, if he'd be a good boy,
20 He'd have God for his father and never want joy.

And so Tom awoke, and we rose in the dark,
And got with our bags and our brushes to work;
Though the morning was cold, Tom was happy and warm –
So if all do their duty, they need not fear harm.

The Little Boy Lost

This poem and the next should be read together. In these poems, Blake continues to develop the theme of true – and false – guardians: the boy is led astray in the first poem to be rescued by a benign God in the second.

8 *And away the vapour flew* – the father is seen as a ghostly figure, a will-o'-the-wisp (marsh gas), leading the boy astray.

Why do you think the father is depicted as a 'vapour'?

Compare the qualities of this 'father' with those of The Shepherd *(page 3).*

The Little Boy Found

The continuation of the story shows the child rescued by God in the guise of his father. This is because Blake wished to underline his belief that true divinity resides only in the hearts of human beings (see *The Marriage of Heaven and Hell*, line 284: 'God only acts and is in existing beings or men').

2 *the wand'ring light* – the vapour, or will-o'-the-wisp, of the preceding poem; now perhaps the emphasis is more on false religion, or misleading ideas.

What is the difference between the father as will-o'-the-wisp and the 'father in white' of this poem?

What is the mother's rôle in the poem?

The Little Boy Lost

'Father, father, where are you going?
Oh do not walk so fast!
Speak, father, speak to your little boy
Or else I shall be lost.'

5   The night was dark, no father was there,
The child was wet with dew;
The mire was deep, and the child did weep,
And away the vapour flew.

The Little Boy Found

The little boy lost in the lonely fen,
Led by the wand'ring light,
Began to cry; but God, ever nigh,
Appeared like his father in white.

5   He kissed the child, and by the hand led,
And to his mother brought,
Who in sorrow pale, through the lonely dale
Her little boy weeping sought.

Laughing Song

Another poem which links human happiness with nature. It is thought that Blake used to sing his poems to tunes he had composed, although none of the music survives. This would seem to be a poem meant to be sung.

6 *grasshopper* – while the grasshopper seems innocuous here, it represents elsewhere in Blake's writings a malign presence.

7 *Mary and Susan and Emily* – common names meant to anchor this pastoral poem in ordinary life.

Who do you think is speaking here?

What are the sources – in rhythm, imagery and diction – of the sense of universal joy in this poem? What is the effect of the grasshopper's presence on this?

Laughing Song

When the green woods laugh with the voice of joy,
And the dimpling stream runs laughing by;
When the air does laugh with our merry wit,
And the green hill laughs with the noise of it;

5   When the meadows laugh with lively green,
And the grasshopper laughs in the merry scene;
When Mary and Susan and Emily
With their sweet round mouths sing 'Ha, ha, he!'

When the painted birds laugh in the shade,
10 Where our table with cherries and nuts is spread,
Come live and be merry, and join with me,
To sing the sweet chorus of 'Ha, ha, he!'

A Cradle Song

For the young Blake, night was a time of terror and nightmare. In this beautiful poem he offers the perfect antidote to those anxieties.

4   *By* – revealed by, or simply, with.

12   *beguiles* – charms away the long night.

15   *Sweet moans, sweeter smiles* – the child's sighs evoke the mother's smiles.

20   *thy mother weep* – for joy; compare the child who weeps to hear the piper in *Introduction*.

22   *image* – the sleeping baby's face reflects the divinity of Jesus.

A Cradle Song

Sweet dreams, form a shade
O'er my lovely infant's head;
Sweet dreams of pleasant streams
By happy, silent, moony beams.

5 Sweet sleep, with soft down
Weave thy brows an infant crown;
Sweet sleep, angel mild,
Hover o'er my happy child.

Sweet smiles in the night
10 Hover over my delight;
Sweet smiles, mother's smiles,
All the livelong night beguiles.

Sweet moans, dovelike sighs,
Chase not slumber from thy eyes;
15 Sweet moans, sweeter smiles,
All the dovelike moans beguiles.

Sleep, sleep, happy child,
All creation slept and smiled;
Sleep, sleep, happy sleep,
20 While o'er thee thy mother weep.

Sweet babe, in thy face,
Holy image I can trace;
Sweet babe, once like thee,
Thy maker lay and wept for me;

What precisely is it about the relationship depicted here which can charm away the terrors of the night?

How does Blake transform the particular picture of mother and child into a vision of a universe of love and harmony?

The Divine Image

In this poem Blake again asserts that divinity is to be found in every human being, regardless of race or creed: when we pray, we do so not to God but to our best selves, for God is in us. The contrary poem to this in **Songs of Experience** is The Human Abstract.

12 *dress* – the body.
13 *clime* – country.

How precisely does God reveal himself in human beings?

What poetic devices does Blake use to emphasize his message in this poem?

25 Wept for me, for thee, for all,
When he was an infant small;
Thou his image ever see,
Heavenly face that smiles on thee –

Smiles on thee, on me, on all,
30 Who became an infant small:
Infant smiles are his own smiles;
Heaven and earth to peace beguiles.

The Divine Image

To Mercy, Pity, Peace and Love
All pray in their distress;
And to these virtues of delight
Return their thankfulness.

5 For Mercy, Pity, Peace and Love
Is God our Father dear;
And Mercy, Pity, Peace and Love
Is man, his child and care.

For Mercy has a human heart,
10 Pity, a human face,
And Love, the human form divine,
And Peace, the human dress.

Then every man of every clime
That prays in his distress,
15 Prays to the human form divine –
Love, Mercy, Pity, Peace.

And all must love the human form
In heathen, Turk, or Jew;
Where Mercy, Love and Pity dwell
20 There God is dwelling too.

Holy Thursday

This poem refers to the custom of marching the children of the London charity schools to St Paul's Cathedral on the first Thursday in May for an annual service instituted in 1782. Compare the poem with that of the same title in **Songs of Experience**.

2   *red and blue and green* – the children are wearing uniforms.

3   *beadles* – parish officers whose rôle was to keep order.
    wands – staffs, or symbols of authority.

5   *a multitude* – as many as 4000-5000 children were involved.
    flowers – i.e. the children.

11 *wise guardians of the poor* – governors or patrons of the charity schools.

12 *Then cherish ... door* – compare 'Be not forgetful to entertain strangers: for thereby some have entertained angels unaware' (*Hebrews*, 13,2).

How does Blake view these 'guardians' in the light of similar figures in poems you have read so far?

Identify the ways in which Blake contrasts the adults with the children.

Holy Thursday

'Twas on a Holy Thursday, their innocent faces clean,
The children walking two and two in red and blue and green,
Grey-headed beadles walked before, with wands as white as snow,
Till into the high dome of Paul's they like Thames' waters flow.

5   Oh what a multitude they seemed, these flowers of London town!
Seated in companies they sit, with radiance all their own;
The hum of multitudes was there, but multitudes of lambs –
Thousands of little boys and girls raising their innocent hands.

Now like a mighty wind they raise to heaven the voice of song,
10 Or like harmonious thunderings the seats of heaven among;
Beneath them sit the aged men, wise guardians of the poor;
Then cherish pity, lest you drive an angel from your door.

Night

A key poem in Blake's developing interest in guardians good and bad: here guardian angels are protective of all forms of life. And when their protection fails, the angels conduct the souls of the dead to heaven. The poem concludes with Blake's vision of eternity, when the lion shall lie down with the lamb.

6   *bower* – a shady nook in a garden (note the reference to the moon as a flower).

9   *Farewell* – as night falls.

13   *pour blessing* – the protective influence of the angels.

> *What do you understand by 'thoughtless nest' in line 17?*

Night

The sun descending in the west,
The evening star does shine;
The birds are silent in their nest,
And I must seek for mine.
5 The moon like a flower
In heaven's high bower,
With silent delight
Sits and smiles on the night.

Farewell, green fields and happy groves,
10 Where flocks have took delight;
Where lambs have nibbled, silent moves
The feet of angels bright;
Unseen they pour blessing
And joy without ceasing
15 On each bud and blossom
And each sleeping bosom.

They look in every thoughtless nest
Where birds are covered warm,
They visit caves of every beast
20 To keep them all from harm.
If they see any weeping
That should have been sleeping,
They pour sleep on their head
And sit down by their bed.

25 *wolves and tigers* – to be seen not just as predatory animals but as the temptations of the world.

26 *stand and weep* – the angels are sometimes ineffective as nature takes its course.

27 *thirst* – bloodlust.

37 *his* – Christ's.

40 *immortal day* – in the new world of heaven, both night and death are absent.

41-2 *And now ... sleep* – compare Isaiah's account (9,7) of Christ's coming kingdom: 'The wolf also shall dwell with the lamb, and the leopard shall lie down with the kid; and the calf and the young lion and the fatling together; and a little child shall lead them.'

43 *him who bore your name* – Jesus is the Lamb of God.

44 *graze* – eat grass.

45 *life's river* – alludes to the religious symbolism of water (provider of life; also cleansing and healing).

What evidence can you find in this poem of Blake's healthy awareness of the normal processes of life and death in nature? What, then, are the implications of 'graze' in line 44?

25 When wolves and tigers howl for prey
They pitying stand and weep,
Seeking to drive their thirst away
And keep them from the sheep;
But if they rush dreadful,
30 The angels most heedful
Receive each mild spirit,
New worlds to inherit.

And there the lion's ruddy eyes
Shall flow with tears of gold,
35 And pitying the tender cries,
And walking round the fold,
Saying: 'Wrath, by his meekness,
And by his health, sickness
Is driven away
40 From our immortal day.

And now beside thee, bleating lamb,
I can lie down and sleep,
Or think on him who bore thy name,
Graze after thee and weep.
45 For, washed in life's river,
My bright mane for ever
Shall shine like the gold
As I guard o'er the fold.'

Spring

This poem celebrates the arrival of spring – and offers a vision of life contrasting with many of the realities of late eighteenth-century England.

Why is the flute suddenly silenced in the second line of the poem?

How does Blake exploit the rhythms of the poem to generate a mood of joy in God's creation?

Spring

      Sound the flute!
      Now it's mute.
      Birds delight
      Day and night;
5   Nightingale
      In the dale,
      Lark in sky,
      Merrily,
      Merrily, merrily, to welcome in the year.

10 Little boy
      Full of joy;
      Little girl
      Sweet and small;
      Cock does crow,
15 So do you;
      Merry voice,
      Infant noise –
      Merrily, merrily, to welcome in the year.

      Little lamb
20 Here I am,
      Come and lick
      My white neck!
      Let me pull
      Your soft wool,
25 Let me kiss
      Your soft face;
      Merrily, merrily, we welcome in the year.

Nurse's Song

Another picture of youthful innocence and happiness, but interestingly this time related by an adult. Compare the poem of the same title in **Songs of Experience**.

How would you describe (and account for) the attitude of mind of the nurse?

What is the effect of the broken rhythm in the last line?

Nurse's Song

When the voices of children are heard on the green
And laughing is heard on the hill,
My heart is at rest within my breast
And everything else is still.

5   'Then come home, my children, the sun is gone down
And the dews of night arise;
Come, come, leave off play, and let us away
Till the morning appears in the skies.'

'No, no! Let us play, for it is yet day
10   And we cannot go to sleep;
Besides, in the sky, the little birds fly
And the hills are all covered with sheep.'

'Well, well, go and play till the light fades away
And then go home to bed.'
15   The little ones leaped and shouted and laughed
And all the hills echoed.

Infant Joy

This poem appears to depict a simple innocent love between mother and newborn baby. Some readings have highlighted the anomaly of the two-day-old child having the power of speech. Compare *Infant Sorrow* in **Songs of Experience**.

5 *Joy* – not used as a Christian name in Blake's time.

How does the poem deal with the ambiguity of the word 'joy'?

In what way might this poem suggest that innocence is a perilous condition?

Infant Joy

'I have no name,
I am but two days old.'
What shall I call thee?
'I happy am,
5 Joy is my name.'
Sweet joy befall thee!

Pretty joy!
Sweet joy but two days old,
Sweet joy I call thee;
10 Thou dost smile,
I sing the while,
Sweet joy befall thee!

A Dream

Blake's 'threefold vision' (see page 148) envisaged an ideal world which we sometimes glimpse in dreams. Interestingly this world still includes loss and separation but the emphasis falls on 'everything that lives is holy' (*The Marriage of Heaven and Hell*, line 486).

1 *weave a shade* – throw a covering (or illusion) over.

2 *angel-guarded bed* – a protected – even enchanted – refuge.

3 *emmet* – ant.

5 *wildered* – lost.

6 *benighted* – stranded out of doors after nightfall.

15 *wight* – creature.

20 *hie thee* – go quickly.

What significance in the light of earlier poems do you find in 'watchman of the night'?

What is the significance of the vision for the human condition?

A Dream

Once a dream did weave a shade
O'er my angel-guarded bed,
That an emmet lost its way
Where on grass methought I lay.

5   Troubled, wildered, and forlorn,
Dark, benighted, travel-worn,
Over many a tangled spray
All heart-broke I heard her say:

'Oh my children! Do they cry?
10 Do they hear their father sigh?
Now they look abroad to see;
Now return and weep for me.'

Pitying, I dropped a tear;
But I saw a glow-worm near
15 Who replied, 'What wailing wight
Calls the watchman of the night?

I am set to light the ground
While the beetle goes his round;
Follow now the beetle's hum –
20 Little wanderer, hie thee home.'

On Another's Sorrow

Blake understands that grief (or loss or separation or death) will never be eradicated from human experience, but here he asserts the consolation that can be found in human compassion and God's goodness.

13   *He who smiles on all* – Jesus.

On Another's Sorrow

Can I see another's woe
And not be in sorrow too?
Can I see another's grief,
And not seek for kind relief?

5   Can I see a falling tear
And not feel my sorrow's share?
Can a father see his child
Weep, nor be with sorrow filled?

Can a mother sit and hear
10 An infant groan, an infant fear?
No, no! never can it be!
Never, never can it be!

And can He who smiles on all,
Hear the wren with sorrows small,
15 Hear the small bird's grief and care,
Hear the woes that infants bear –

And not sit beside the nest
Pouring pity in their breast?
And not sit the cradle near
20 Weeping tear on infant's tear?

And not sit both night and day
Wiping all our tears away?
Oh no! never can it be!
Never, never can it be!

26 *an infant small* – Jesus took human form when he came to earth.

28 *He doth feel the sorrow too* – i.e. at the crucifixion.

30 *maker* – God incarnate as Jesus.

Could it be argued that Blake's assertions raise doubts about the extent of human compassion?

The poem looks forward to the ending of suffering when Christ comes into his Kingdom. How does the poem evoke a more immediate and earthly consolation?

25   He doth give his joy to all,
      He becomes an infant small;
      He becomes a man of woe,
      He doth feel the sorrow too.

      Think not thou canst sigh a sigh
30   And thy maker is not by;
      Think not thou canst weep a tear
      And thy maker is not near.

      Oh! he gives to us his joy
      That our grief he may destroy;
35   Till our grief is fled and gone
      He doth sit by us and moan.

Songs of Experience

Introduction

Introduction should be read in conjunction with *Earth's Answer*. It seems to suggest that there is hope for mankind, in spite of the corruption in the world which subsequent poems in this section describe. Critics are divided over whether the bard, who is thought to be Blake, endorses or contradicts the Holy Word in his call for personal and social renewal.

1   *bard* – a poet/prophet who sees hope for the future but also the evils of the present.

4   *Holy Word* – to be identified with Jehovah, God of the Old Testament.

5   *ancient trees* – in the Garden of Eden.

6   *lapsed soul* – Adam (and Eve), i.e. morally fallen.

9   *starry pole* – sky, but also a symbol of Newtonian rationalism.

10 *fallen, fallen light renew* – i.e. the fallen soul can only perceive a false image of salvation.

11 *Earth* – a symbol of fallen humanity.

15 *slumberous mass* – another image representing a world view founded on Newtonian physics.

18 *starry floor* – the night sky but again a symbol of the rigid rational order of the Newtonian universe.

19 *wat'ry shore* – the material world of time and space.

20 *break of day* – a new world order, presided over by the Jesus of the New Testament; compare Blake's hopes for the American and French Revolutions.

Trace the contrast between the outlook of the bard and the Holy Word.

Why does the earth turn away?

Songs of Experience

Introduction

Hear the voice of the bard!
Who present, past and future sees;
Whose ears have heard
The Holy Word
5 That walked among the ancient trees

Calling the lapsed soul,
And weeping in the evening dew;
That might control
The starry pole,
10 And fallen, fallen light renew!

'Oh Earth, oh Earth, return!
Arise from out the dewy grass;
Night is worn,
And the morn
15 Rises from the slumberous mass.

Turn away no more!
Why wilt thou turn away?
The starry floor,
The wat'ry shore,
20 Is giv'n thee till the break of day.'

Earth's Answer

In this poem, the Earth explains why she is not able on her own to renew the fallen light: she is enslaved by reason, law and restriction. The bard sees his rôle as releasing the Earth from the chains of false ideologies and promoting compassion, freedom and love.

3   *Her light fled* – i.e. her vitality extinct.

4   *Stony dread* – paralysed with fear.

7   *Starry Jealousy* – a personification depicting the all-inclusive nature of the rationalist outlook.

8   *hoar* – frosty (by implication, white-haired)

10   *the father of the ancient men* – possibly the Holy Word of *Introduction*; a restrictive father/God figure and the God of Reason envisaged by Newton.

13   *delight* – imagination, instinct, freedom, intuition: a spontaneous expression.

•

21   *chain* – a restrictive moral code which emphasizes rationality at the expense of love and happiness.

24   *bane* – source or cause of evil or destruction.

How does Blake emphasize in this poem the unnaturalness of a fallen world?

Is the poem completely without hope?

Earth's Answer

Earth raised up her head
From the darkness, dread and drear;
Her light fled,
Stony dread!
5   And her locks covered with grey despair.

'Prisoned on wat'ry shore,
Starry Jealousy does keep my den:
Cold and hoar,
Weeping o'er,
10   I hear the father of the ancient men.

Selfish father of men!
Cruel, jealous, selfish fear!
Can delight
Chained in night
15   The virgins of youth and morning bear?

Does spring hide its joy
When buds and blossoms grow?
Does the sower
Sow by night,
20   Or the ploughman in darkness plough?

Break this heavy chain
That does freeze my bones around! –
Selfish, vain,
Eternal bane!
25   That free love with bondage bound.'

The Clod and the Pebble

Critical debate on this poem has centred on whether the clod or the pebble is right about the nature of love, and where Blake's sympathies lie.

7 *brook* – water is often a symbol of materialism in Blake.

8 *metres* – here, the next stanza, but strictly the rhythmic pattern of a line of poetry.
meet – suitable, appropriate.

12 *despite* – in spite of; as a noun, with general connotations of ill-will, malice or hatred.

Are the positions of both clod and pebble equally extreme? Does Blake value one over the other?

Why does Blake employ a clod and a pebble to explore the nature of love in the world of experience?

The Clod and the Pebble

'Love seeketh not itself to please,
Nor for itself hath any care;
But for another gives its ease
And builds a heaven in hell's despair.'

5   So sung a little clod of clay,
Trodden with the cattle's feet,
But a pebble of the brook
Warbled out these metres meet:

'Love seeketh only self to please,
10 To bind another to its delight;
Joys in another's loss of ease,
And builds a hell in heaven's despite.'

Holy Thursday

For the context of this poem, refer to the notes on the contrary poem in **Songs of Innocence**. This poem expresses a much more explicit indignation towards a social abuse.

1   *holy* – Blake is astonished that a supposedly religious nation can tolerate such things.

4   *usurous* – strictly, usury refers to charging exorbitant interest on loans, but Blake has in mind the hypocritical prestige the guardians of the poor gain from a public show of their charitable work.
    hand – i.e. of 'the wise guardians of the poor'.

13   *where'er the sun does shine* – a vision of a just society.

What are the full implications of line 8: 'It is a land of poverty!'?

What effect does Blake achieve by the contrasts he reveals in the third and fourth stanzas?

Holy Thursday

Is this a holy thing to see
In a rich and fruitful land?
Babes reduced to misery,
Fed with cold and usurous hand?

5   Is that trembling cry a song?
Can it be a song of joy?
And so many children poor?
It is a land of poverty!

And their sun does never shine,
10 And their fields are bleak and bare,
And their ways are filled with thorns –
It is eternal winter there.

For where'er the sun does shine
And where'er the rain does fall,
15 Babe can never hunger there,
Nor poverty the mind appal.

The Little Girl Lost

This and the next poem should be read together. Both these poems appeared originally in **Songs of Innocence**. They echo myths (e.g. Persephone) affirming the cycle of the seasons and the return of fertility at the end of winter. Lyca could be seen as an allegorical figure from a paradise, who is drawn to self-sacrifice in order to ensure the renewal of Earth prophesied by the bard. At another level, the poems have been read as being about the dawning of human sexuality.

4   *grave* – engrave (verb), i.e. the prophet's words should be noted; or, serious (adjective), i.e. the punishment suffered by a fallen world (sleep).

8   *garden mild* – the Garden of Eden will be restored in a redeemed world by Lyca's sacrifice.

The Little Girl Lost

In futurity
I prophetic see
That the earth from sleep
(Grave the sentence deep)

5 Shall arise and seek
For her maker meek,
And the desert wild
Become a garden mild.

In the southern clime,
10 Where the summer's prime
Never fades away,
Lovely Lyca lay.

Seven summers old
Lovely Lyca told;
15 She had wandered long
Hearing wild birds' song.

'Sweet sleep, come to me
Underneath this tree;
Do father, mother weep?
20 Where can Lyca sleep?

Lost in desert wild
Is your little child;
How can Lyca sleep
If her mother weep?

25 If her heart does ache
Then let Lyca wake;
If my mother sleep
Lyca shall not weep.

50   *slender dress* – as a fertility goddess Lyca gives up her physical body in order to regenerate the earth.

How does Blake link Lyca's experience with a vision of a restored earthly paradise?

How could this be seen as an exploration of Lyca's sexual awakening?

Frowning, frowning night,
30   O'er this desert bright,
Let thy moon arise
While I close my eyes.'

Sleeping Lyca lay
While the beasts of prey,
35   Come from caverns deep,
Viewed the maid asleep.

The kingly lion stood
And the virgin viewed,
The he gambolled round
40   O'er the hallowed ground.

Leopards, tigers play,
Round her as she lay,
While the lion old
Bowed his mane of gold

45   And her bosom lick,
And upon her neck
From his eyes of flame
Ruby tears there came;

While the lioness
50   Loosed her slender dress,
And naked they conveyed
To caves the sleeping maid.

The Little Girl Found

Here the attention switches to the anxieties of the parents for their 'lost' child. The meeting with the lion/spirit reassures them of her rôle in the regeneration of the earth.

14   *the fancied image* – i.e. the parents are determined to see Lyca as in danger.

18   *pressed* – probably, was rooted to the spot.

22   *armed* – the word suggests the harm which misplaced sorrow or anxiety can do to the innocent.

The Little Girl Found

All the night in woe
Lyca's parents go;
Over valleys deep,
While the deserts weep.

5 Tired and woe-begone,
Hoarse with making moan,
Arm in arm seven days
They traced the desert ways.

Seven nights they sleep
10 Among shadows deep,
And dream they see their child
Starved in desert wild.

Pale through pathless ways
The fancied image strays –
15 Famished, weeping, weak,
With hollow piteous shriek.

Rising from unrest,
The trembling woman pressed
With feet of weary woe;
20 She could no further go.

In his arms he bore
Her, armed with sorrow sore;
Till before their way
A couching lion lay.

25 Turning back was vain;
Soon his heavy mane
Bore them to the ground;
Then he stalked around

30   *allay* – subside, diminish.

45   *followed* – three syllables.

Look carefully at the lion/spirit. What does Blake intend by the terms of this description?

What is the nature of the reassurance that the parents gain? Why do they spend the rest of their lives in a 'lonely dell'?

Smelling to his prey.
30 But their fears allay
When he licks their hands,
And silent by them stands.

They look upon his eyes
Filled with deep surprise,
35 And wondering behold
A spirit armed in gold.

On his head a crown,
On his shoulders down
Flowed his golden hair;
40 Gone was all their care.

'Follow me,' he said,
'Weep not for the maid;
In my palace deep
Lyca lies asleep.'

45 Then they followed
Where the vision led,
And saw their sleeping child
Among tigers wild.

To this day they dwell
50 In a lonely dell;
Nor fear the wolvish howl,
Nor the lion's growl.

The Chimney Sweeper

In the contrary poem in **Songs of Innocence**, the boy was consoled by simple platitudes: here there are no such illusions. The boy is bitterly aware of the way his parents have betrayed him, and consciously seeks to evoke the listener's sympathy.

2   *weep* – street call asking for work, also 'notes of woe'.

12   *heaven* – an illusion based on ignoring the suffering around them, including the exploitation of children.

> How does the parents' attitude serve to forward Blake's attack on the authorities of Church and State?

> Is this child of experience better or worse off than the child in the companion poem in **Songs of Innocence**?

Nurse's Song

Unlike the contrary poem in **Songs of Innocence**, there is only one voice here – that of the disillusioned nurse. Her analysis of the situation and the finality of her conclusions mark this as the voice of experience.

2   *whisp'rings ... in the dale* – furtive amorous encounters.

4   *green and pale* – significant of destructive envy.

7   *wasted in play* – the nurse considers there are better ways for the children to spend their time.

> Is the nurse merely saddened by the short-lived nature of children's innocence, or is she so jaundiced that she wishes to deny to others what she has herself lost?

> What does the last line mean? Relate it to the 'whisp'rings ... in the dale'.

The Chimney Sweeper

A little black thing among the snow,
Crying 'weep, weep' in notes of woe;
'Where are thy father and mother, say?'
'They are both gone up to the church to pray.

5   Because I was happy upon the heath
And smiled among the winter's snow,
They clothed me in the clothes of death,
And taught me to sing the notes of woe.

And because I am happy and dance and sing,
10   They think they have done me no injury,
And are gone to praise God and his priest and king,
Who make up a heaven of our misery.'

Nurse's Song

When the voices of children are heard on the green
And whisp'rings are in the dale,
The days of my youth rise fresh in my mind,
My face turns green and pale.

5   Then come home, my children, the sun is gone down,
And the dews of night arise;
Your spring and your day are wasted in play,
And your winter and night in disguise.

The Sick Rose

It would be a mistake to attempt to pin down the meaning of this poem too precisely. Blake merges traditional symbolism with his own symbol system. Thus, if the rose is seen as a symbol of love and the worm as a symbol of corruption, Blake may be commenting on the threats to human relationships. Some commentators have also suggested that the worm might represent the Church, i.e. the authority that puts marriage before love: Blake thought that most of the population had been 'seduced' by the false and life-denying doctrines of an insidious Church. You could compare the suggested contrary poem *The Blossom* in **Songs of Innocence** to sharpen your perceptions of this poem.

Overall structure and word order are key elements in this poem. What would you pick out as significant and what is the effect gained?

Compare this poem with The Blossom. *What is it about the world of experience which corrupts? What is lost?*

The Sick Rose

Oh rose, thou art sick;
The invisible worm,
That flies in the night
In the howling storm,

5   Has found out thy bed
Of crimson joy,
And his dark secret love
Does thy life destroy.

The Fly

In many of the **Songs of Experience** the voice we hear is that of experience with all its limitations. Therefore, we need to be even more careful than in **Songs of Innocence** not simply to identify the speaker with Blake. While reading this poem, remember that Blake believed in human divinity (God-in-man) and that 'everything that lives is holy'.

What features of the poem (form as well as content) suggest that this is not Blake speaking?

In view of what you now know about Blake, how adequate are the conclusions of the poem?

The Fly

Little fly,
Thy summer's play
My thoughtless hand
Has brushed away.

5 Am not I
A fly like thee?
Or art not thou
A man like me?

For I dance
10 And drink and sing
Till some blind hand
Shall brush my wing.

If thought is life
And strength and breath,
15 And the want
of thought is death,

Then am I
A happy fly,
If I live
20 Or if I die.

The Angel

This is a poem that shows how human beings can put up barriers to love by denying their natural instincts, represented here by the angel.

4   *Witless ... beguiled* – the affectation of a sentimental love made her unable to respond fully to the angel's overtures and listen to her instincts.

8   *hid from him my heart's delight* – the repression of the expression of her true feelings.

10   *the morn blushed rosy red* – blushes are always a sign of corruption in Blake.

12   *shields and spears* – symbols of sexual vitality and her desire.

16   *grey hairs* – not necessarily old, but now having the characteristics of old age.

Try to recount this narrative in your own words.

How successfully does Blake transform the angel into a human lover?

The Angel

I dreamt a dream! What can it mean?
And that I was a maiden queen
Guarded by an angel mild:
Witless woe was ne'er beguiled!

5 And I wept both night and day,
And he wiped my tears away,
And I wept both day and night,
And hid from him my heart's delight.

So he took his wings and fled,
10 Then the morn blushed rosy red;
I dried my tears and armed my fears
With ten thousand shields and spears.

Soon my angel came again:
I was armed, he came in vain –
15 For the time of youth was fled,
And grey hairs were on my head.

The Tiger

This is perhaps Blake's most famous poem and it has attracted a great deal of interest and critical response. Apart from looking at the obvious contrary poem in **Songs of Innocence** (*The Lamb*), which this poem positively invites you to do, you should perhaps also take another look at *Night* and the representation of tigers there.

2   *forests of the night* – both night and forest are symbols of oppression in Blake.

4   *frame* – conceive: an act of creation and production.

7   *dare* – the audacity to act.

8   *seize the fire* – the gift of fire was jealously guarded by the gods, in Greek mythology, but Prometheus braved their wrath to bring it to earth for the benefit of mankind.

9   *shoulder* – i.e. requiring strength as well as skill.

12   *What dread hand, and what dread feet?* – i.e. fashioned the heart.

17   *stars* – Satan and the fallen angels, who wept as they conceded defeat.

19-20   *Did he smile ... make thee?* – After the fall of the angels, God created the world and all its creatures (and smiled, i.e. he 'saw that it was good', *Genesis*, 1,25); did the same God make both meek and strong?

Identify the central image used by Blake to describe the creation of the tiger. Why is it appropriate?

What is the answer to the question posed in line 20? What is Blake's attitude towards the tiger?

The Tiger

Tiger, tiger, burning bright
In the forests of the night,
What immortal hand or eye
Could frame thy fearful symmetry?

5 In what distant deeps or skies
Burnt the fire of thine eyes?
On what wings dare he aspire?
What the hand dare seize the fire?

And what shoulder, and what art,
10 Could twist the sinews of thy heart?
And when thy heart began to beat,
What dread hand and what dread feet?

What the hammer? What the chain?
In what furnace was thy brain?
15 What the anvil? What dread grasp
Dare its deadly terrors clasp?

When the stars threw down their spears
And watered heaven with their tears,
Did he smile his work to see?
20 Did he who made the lamb make thee?

Tiger, tiger, burning bright
In the forests of the night,
What immortal hand or eye
Dare frame thy fearful symmetry?

My Pretty Rose-Tree

It is possible that this poem derived from a personal experience of Blake's. The story goes that he rejected the overtures of another woman, but instead of applauding his constancy, his wife Kate nevertheless was jealous. Blake saw this as her wish – sanctioned by the marriage contract – to possess his sexual liberty, and an echo therefore of the commercial morality of the times which he hated.

 2 *as May never bore* – surpassing the beauty of a May flower.

Does this poem in any way upset the traditional symbolism of the rose?

Can you find any evidence in the poem that the rose tree is right to turn away with jealousy?

Ah, Sunflower!

The sunflower's bending to follow the path of the sun is likened to a longing for a golden world beyond that of experience where sexuality will not be compromised by lust and inhibition.

 3 *clime* – country.

How would you describe the tone of this poem? Does Blake see the desirable state described as attainable – or an illusory hope?

There is something odd about the grammar of this poem. Can you find what it is? What is its effect?

The Lily

You may well wonder what this poem is doing in **Songs of Experience**. The lily 'delights' in love while the rose and the sheep seem to be more defensive. Have another look at the previous poem, where Blake envisages a time when sexuality takes its proper place in an innocent world.

 3 *lily* – traditionally a symbol of purity.

What new meanings are the familiar images of the rose and the sheep given in this poem?

Does this take the vision of the two previous poems further?

My Pretty Rose-Tree

A flower was offered to me,
Such a flower as May never bore;
But I said, 'I've a pretty rose-tree',
And I passed the sweet flower o'er.

5   Then I went to my pretty rose-tree
To tend her by day and by night;
But my rose turned away with jealousy
And her thorns were my only delight.

Ah, Sunflower!

Ah, sunflower! weary of time,
Who countest the steps of the sun,
Seeking after that sweet golden clime
Where the traveller's journey is done;

5   Where the youth pined away with desire,
And the pale virgin shrouded in snow,
Arise from their graves and aspire
Where my sunflower wishes to go.

The Lily

The modest rose puts forth a thorn,
The humble sheep a threat'ning horn;
While the lily white shall in love delight,
Nor a thorn nor a threat stain her beauty bright.

The Garden of Love

The contrary poem in **Songs of Innocence** is *The Echoing Green*. Here the green, the place of childhood play, has been corrupted by a repressive religious morality.

6   *'Thou shalt not'* – a reference to the Ten Commandments.

Blake's idea of love is contrasted in this poem with that of the Church of England. Summarize and compare these ideas. It might help to review the previous poems.

The rhythm employed in this poem is the same as that in The Echoing Green. *What effects does Blake achieve here by its use?*

The Garden of Love

I went to the Garden of Love
And saw what I never had seen:
A chapel was built in the midst,
Where I used to play on the green.

5   And the gates of this chapel were shut,
And 'Thou shalt not' writ over the door;
So I turned to the Garden of Love
That so many sweet flowers bore,

And I saw it was filled with graves
10 And tombstones where flowers should be;
And priests in black gowns were walking their rounds,
And binding with briars my joys and desires.

The Little Vagabond

As in the preceding poem, the central attack here is on the Church of England's lack of humanity and warmth. This poem was suppressed when **Songs of Innocence and of Experience** was first published commercially in 1839, because it was considered subversive.

4   *usage* – treatment.

6   *regale* – entertain, please.

11   *modest Dame Lurch* – a schoolmistress, or an inadequate mother (who leaves her children 'in the lurch').

12   *bandy* – i.e. with curving legs caused by rickets, a vitamin deficiency disease.
      nor fasting nor birch – methods of punishment.

15   *barrel* – i.e. of ale.

16   *give him both drink and apparel* – the Church would no longer reject the vagabond but welcome him (with refreshment and clothing) in the same way that the Prodigal Son was greeted by his father (*Luke*, 15, 11-32).

Consider the voice of the poem. How do you account for its inclusion in **Songs of Experience**?

Why might the Victorians in particular have found this poem so offensive?

The Little Vagabond

Dear mother, dear mother, the church is cold
But the alehouse is healthy and pleasant and warm;
Besides I can tell where I am used well –
Such usage in heaven will never do well.

5   But if at the church they would give us some ale,
And a pleasant fire our souls to regale,
We'd sing and we'd pray all the livelong day,
Nor ever once wish from the church to stray.

Then the parson might preach and drink and sing,
10   And we'd be as happy as birds in the spring;
And modest Dame Lurch, who is always at church,
Would not have bandy children nor fasting nor birch.

And God, like a father rejoicing to see
His children as pleasant and happy as he,
15   Would have no more quarrel with the devil or the barrel
But kiss him and give him both drink and apparel.

London

In this poem Blake invites the reader to reassess current social values. He seems to argue that the new freedoms and rights of the emerging modern society are, paradoxically, leading to hardship for many and unhappiness for all. The poem concludes with a horrifying vision of social degeneration.

1, 2   *chartered* – a bill of rights, a royal document giving legal status to a city, a legal contract, a map, a legal constraint, a guarantee; compare 'the cheating ways of chartered streams' in *Why should I care for the men of Thames* (page 131).

3   *mark* – notice, (re)mark.

7   *ban* – curse or swear-word, with possibly a reference also to a legal prohibition.

8   *manacles* – handcuffs (metaphorically, to control the mind).

9   *chimney-sweeper's cry* – i.e. 'weep, weep'.

10   *black'ning* – as well as the obvious physical consequences of industrialization, the moral irresponsibility of the Church in the matter of social evils.
    appals – strictly, horrifies; but with the sense of casting a black funeral pall of soot over the moribund Church.

11   *hapless* – unfortunate.

12   *palace* – the tyranny of monarchy (particularly of George III).

14   *harlot's curse* – strictly, venereal disease carried by the prostitute – but be careful to avoid too literal an interpretation. Compare the 'blood that runs down palace walls', i.e. the horrors which are descending on this civilization.

15-16   *Blasts ... blights* – the husband infected with venereal disease by a prostitute can pass it to both wife and child; the words are often applied to diseased flowers and plants (and this should again alert you to the need to avoid too literal an interpretation of the metaphors).

Consider the full implications of Blake's use of the word 'chartered' to describe the Thames and streets of London: does he use the word favourably or not? Is he exploiting conflicting meanings of the word? Look up the words of Rule Britannia, *written in 1740.*

What do you understand by the phrase 'mind-forged manacles'? How does this condition afflict the victims as well as the oppressors?

London

I wander through each chartered street
Near where the chartered Thames does flow,
And mark in every face I meet
Marks of weakness, marks of woe.

5   In every cry of every man,
In every infant's cry of fear,
In every voice, in every ban,
The mind-forged manacles I hear.

How the chimney-sweeper's cry
10 Every black'ning church appals,
And the hapless soldier's sigh
Runs in blood down palace walls.

But most through midnight streets I hear
How the youthful harlot's curse
15 Blasts the new-born infant's tear,
And blights with plagues the marriage hearse.

The Human Abstract

The contrary poem in **Songs of Innocence** is *The Divine Image*. This is an impressive poem which economically shows the susceptibility of human nature to evil and corruption and how those vices flourish and become institutionalized in a society. Governance and religion based on abstract reasoning are able to distance themselves from what is going on in the real world.

5   *mutual fear brings peace* – probably in the sense of a social contract, under which members of a society agree to laws which restrict individual freedoms in order to protect the safety of all.

9   *holy fears* – fear of God can be a sign of the devout life, but Blake is being ironic as in his view the Church of England is an institution to be feared.

14   *Mystery* – again, mystery can be a divine truth, but Blake's image of a tree of mystery suggests religious oppression (note also the reference to the Tree of Knowledge in the Garden of Eden in the following lines).

15   *the caterpillar and the fly* – symbols for the clergy.

19   *raven* – a bird of ill-omen and death.

22   *this tree* – perhaps a reference to the fabled upas tree which brought death to any living thing which came near it; of course, no such tree was ever found, but Blake suggests that this is because it exists in the human mind, not in nature.

What precisely is Blake saying about pity and mercy in the first stanza?

How does Blake develop and illustrate his notion of 'mind-forged manacles' here?

The Human Abstract

Pity would be no more
If we did not make somebody poor;
And Mercy no more could be,
If all were as happy as we.

5 And mutual fear brings peace
Till the selfish loves increase;
Then Cruelty knits a snare
And spreads his baits with care.

He sits down with holy fears
10 And waters the ground with tears;
Then Humility takes its root
Underneath his foot.

Soon spreads the dismal shade
Of Mystery over his head,
15 And the caterpillar and fly
Feed on the mystery.

And it bears the fruit of Deceit,
Ruddy and sweet to eat;
And the raven his nest has made
20 In its thickest shade.

The gods of the earth and sea
Sought through nature to find this tree,
But their search was all in vain –
There grows one in the human brain.

Infant Sorrow

This poem emphatically counters the simplicity of *Infant Joy* in **Songs of Innocence**. It is another poem which shows the vulnerability of innocence, or the susceptibility of human nature to corruption, sometimes from unlikely sources.

3   *piping* – the crying of the baby.

4   *Like a fiend hid in a cloud* – this line is a problem: despite the associations – and Blake's use elsewhere of clouds to symbolize corruption or oppression – this is probably a simile which denotes the unsocialized, but natural, instincts of the infant.

6   *swaddling bands* – strips of cloth in which the baby is wrapped (representing mental as well as physical restriction).

Referring back to Infant Joy, *to what extent does the initial reaction of the parents account for the different responses of the children?*

What condition is the child in at the end of the poem?

A Poison Tree

This is a poem intended to subvert the idea of 'turning the other cheek': it shows the destructive consequences – for both the offended and offending parties – of suppressing anger. There may again be a reference to the upas tree (see *The Human Abstract*), and to the Tree of Knowledge (*Genesis, 3,3*): 'But of the fruit of the tree which is in the midst of the garden, God hath said, Ye shall not eat of it, neither shall ye touch it, lest ye die.'

7   *sunned* – two syllables.

8   *wiles* – sly tricks.

14   *pole* – the sky.

Why is it important for the narrator that 'he knew that it [the apple] was mine'?

How in terms of the structure of the poem are the inevitable consequences of repressing emotions demonstrated?

Infant Sorrow

> My mother groaned, my father wept!
> Into the dangerous world I leapt:
> Helpless, naked, piping loud
> Like a fiend hid in a cloud.
>
> 5 Struggling in my father's hands,
> Striving against my swaddling bands,
> Bound and weary I thought best
> To sulk upon my mother's breast.

A Poison Tree

> I was angry with my friend;
> I told my wrath, my wrath did end.
> I was angry with my foe;
> I told it not, my wrath did grow.
>
> 5 And I watered it in fears,
> Night and morning with my tears;
> And I sunned it with smiles,
> And with soft deceitful wiles.
>
> And it grew both day and night
> 10 Till it bore an apple bright;
> And my foe beheld it shine,
> And he knew that it was mine.
>
> And into my garden stole
> When the night had veiled the pole –
> 15 In the morning glad I see
> My foe outstretched beneath the tree.

A Little Boy Lost

In this poem, Blake argues that true religion derives from simple humanity and not the esoteric mysteries by which priests exert their power.

2 *venerates* – reveres, looks up to.

10 *zeal* – religious enthusiasm.

15 *reason* – common sense.
16 *mystery* – a divine truth beyond rational explanation.

24 *Albion* – Britain.

The little boy's point of view is endorsed by Blake in other poems elsewhere. What precisely is he saying? How does it compare with the views of the priest?

What evidence can you find in the poem that Blake uses this scenario to express his outrage at the power of priests?

A Little Boy Lost

'Nought loves another as itself,
Nor venerates another so,
Nor is it possible to thought
A greater than itself to know.

5 And, father, how can I love you
Or any of my brothers more?
I love you like the little bird
That picks up crumbs around the door.'

The priest sat by and heard the child,
10 In trembling zeal he seized his hair;
He led him by his little coat
And all admired the priestly care.

And standing on the altar high,
'Lo, what a fiend is here!' said he,
15 'One who sets reason up for judge
Of our most holy mystery.'

The weeping child could not be heard,
The weeping parents wept in vain;
They stripped him to his little shirt
20 And bound him in an iron chain,

And burned him in a holy place
Where many had been burned before.
The weeping parents wept in vain –
Are such things done on Albion's shore?

A Little Girl Lost

This poem is the contrary poem to *The Little Girl Lost* which originally appeared in **Songs of Innocence**. Blake compares the way sexuality is viewed in contemporary society with an ideal age of innocence, 'the age of gold'. Refer back to *Earth's Answer* for a contrasting account of the present age.

6   *winter's cold* – the age of gold should be compared with the Garden of Eden where there were no extremes of temperature.

27   *loving look* – in reality, a look which is meant to terrify.
28   *holy book* – The Bible, but here with an emphasis on the terror of God's law and therefore not holy at all.

A Little Girl Lost

Children of the future age,
Reading this indignant page,
Know that in a former time
Love, sweet love, was thought a crime.

5   In the age of gold,
    Free from winter's cold,
    Youth and maiden bright
    To the holy light,
    Naked in the sunny beams delight.

10 Once a youthful pair
    Filled with softest care
    Met in garden bright,
    Where the holy light
    Had just removed the curtains of the night.

15 There in rising day
    On the grass they play;
    Parents were afar,
    Strangers came not near,
    And the maiden soon forgot her fear.

20 Tired with kisses sweet,
    They agree to meet
    When the silent sleep
    Waves o'er heavens deep,
    And the weary tired wanderers weep.

25 To her father white
    Came the maiden bright,
    But his loving look,
    Like the holy book
    All her tender limbs with terror shook.

30 *Ona* – Blake may be alluding to Una in Spenser's *The Faerie Queene* who represents true religion and is wrongly accused of lechery.

33 *hoary* – white like hoar frost (suggesting age and lack of feeling).

How would you describe the attitude of Ona's father? Pick out the details in the poem which convey this.

Is there anything in the poem which suggests the lovers expected such a response?

To Tirzah

Blake added this poem to **Songs of Experience** at a later date. The poet's mood had darkened and he felt that the false attitudes he had attacked in the earlier poems had been overtaken by the even worse evil of materialism. Essentially, this is what Tirzah represents – a figure who (after the Fall) binds human beings to an earthly existence.

2 *consumed with the earth* – i.e. death, the fate of humanity after the Fall.

3 *generation* – the mortal process by which the earth is peopled.

4 *Then what have I to do with thee?* – compare Christ's words to his mother at the wedding in Cana: 'Woman, what have I to do with thee?' (*John*, 2, 4), i.e. the rejection of the physical body (the earthly mother) in favour of a spiritual rebirth.

5 *The sexes sprung from shame and pride* – these and the following lines should be read as a version of the Fall, the inhibitions and the suffering that followed from it.

6 *Blowed* – bloomed.

9 *mother* – Tirzah, who creates the physical body.

12-13 *nostrils, eyes and ears/.... tongue* – the four physical senses.

15 *The death of Jesus set me free* – probably in the sense of death as a release from the physical body for a spiritual resurrection rather than the more orthodox view of Christ's punishment on the cross being for mankind's sins.

Why is the 'clay' (the physical body) described as 'senseless'?

This is a challenging – in some ways disturbing – poem. How do you respond to its solution to the problems of materialism?

30   'Ona, pale and weak,
      To thy father speak! -
      Oh, the trembling fear!
      Oh, the dismal care
      That shakes the blossoms of my hoary hair!'

To Tirzah

      Whate'er is born of mortal birth
      Must be consumed with the earth
      To rise from generation free;
      Then what have I to do with thee?

5   The sexes sprung from shame and pride –
      Blowed in the morn, in evening died;
      But Mercy changed death into sleep –
      The sexes rose to work and weep.

      Thou mother of my mortal part
10   With cruelty didst mould my heart,
      And with false self-deceiving tears
      Didst bind my nostrils, eyes and ears;

      Didst close my tongue in senseless clay
      And me to mortal life betray:
15   The death of Jesus set me free –
      Then what have I to do with thee?

The Schoolboy

This poem originally appeared in **Songs of Innocence**. It is perhaps easy to see why it was transferred to **Songs of Experience**. Blake resumes his theme showing the vulnerability of innocence. Here the threat is posed by conventional education which Blake, who was educated at home, always distrusted.

3   *winds* – blows.

14   *learning's bower* – probably meant ironically, as a bower usually denotes a place of peaceful seclusion, especially in a garden.

29   *mellowing* – ripening.

> *Blake seems to associate both teacher and parents in the threat to childhood innocence in this poem. What does he see as the nature of that threat?*

> *An extended metaphor from line 21 compares children with plants. What effects does Blake seek through this comparison? What does he identify as the consequences in adulthood of a childhood where 'buds are nipped'?*

The Schoolboy

    I love to rise in a summer morn
    When the birds sing on every tree;
    The distant huntsman winds his horn,
    And the skylark sings with me –
5 Oh, what sweet company!

    But to go to school in a summer morn,
    Oh, it drives all joy away;
    Under a cruel eye outworn,
    The little ones spend the day
10 In sighing and dismay.

    Ah! then at times I drooping sit
    And spend many an anxious hour;
    Nor in my book can I take delight,
    Nor sit in learning's bower,
15 Worn through with the dreary shower.

    How can the bird that is born for joy
    Sit in a cage and sing?
    How can a child, when fears annoy,
    But droop his tender wing
20 And forget his youthful spring?

    Oh, father and mother, if buds are nipped
    And blossoms blown away,
    And if the tender plants are stripped
    Of their joy in the springing day
25 By sorrow and care's dismay,

    How shall the summer arise in joy
    Or the summer fruits appear?
    Or how shall we gather what griefs destroy,
    Or bless the mellowing year
30 When the blasts of winter appear?

The Voice of the Ancient Bard

This poem originally appeared in **Songs of Innocence**. While fully recognizing the perils of the world of experience, the poem nevertheless sounds a note of hope. This therefore contrasts with the tone set in the opening poem of **Songs of Experience**.

2   *opening* – first light.

4   *clouds of reason* – rationalism which obscures rather than illuminates.

Why do you think there is such a dramatic change of rhythm in lines 9–11?

In what ways might the poem be seen as concluding Blake's investigation of wise and false leadership?

The Voice of the Ancient Bard

Youth of delight, come hither
And see the opening morn –
Image of truth new-born;
Doubt is fled, and clouds of reason,
5   Dark disputes and artful teasing.
Folly is an endless maze,
Tangled roots perplex her ways –
How many have fallen there!
They stumble all night over bones of the dead,
10   And feel they know not what but care,
And wish to lead others, when they should be led.

The Marriage of Heaven and Hell

The Marriage of Heaven and Hell (1790-93) belongs to the same period as
Songs of Innocence and of Experience and is an invaluable source for
Blake's ideas and personal philosophy. In some ways it can be seen as his
intellectual and artistic manifesto. At its centre is an assault on rationalism
and materialism and an affirmation of the powers of human imagination. It is
also a satirical attack on the ideas of Emanuel Swedenborg, whose writings
had once influenced Blake; a denunciation of the established Church of
England and conventional religion; and a celebration of the French
Revolution. The Marriage of Heaven and Hell, however, is not open to
straightforward interpretation and readers should be aware of the layers of
meaning in the text. In Blake's original version, the text, written in a
combination of poetry and prose, is incorporated into 27 illustrated plates
(hand-coloured etchings). In the version that follows, these divisions have
been retained to facilitate the commentaries and critical apparatus.

The Argument
Plate 2

This opening section introduces the idea of the 'just man' who, in late
eighteenth-century England, must forsake meekness for righteous
indignation in the face of a compromised and failing Church of England. From
the outset, the poem holds out the promise of revolutionary change.

  1   *Rintrah* – an invented mythological figure representing wrath; the
      natural energies released by the American and French Revolutions.

  2   *swag* – sway.

  5   *The vale of death* – this world.

 14 *the villain* – compare 'the sneaking serpent' in line 17; both are
      references to the clergy of the Church of England.

 16 *barren climes* – the religious and moral malaise of late eighteenth-
      century society.

Why does Rintrah rage?

What does Blake identify as the shortcomings of the clergy?

The Marriage of Heaven and Hell

The Argument
Plate 2

Rintrah roars and shakes his fires in the burdened air;
Hungry clouds swag on the deep.

Once meek, and in a perilous path,
The just man kept his course along
5   The vale of death;
Roses are planted where thorns grow,
And on the barren heath
Sing the honey bees.

Then the perilous path was planted;
10 And a river and a spring
On every cliff and tomb;
And on the bleached bones
Red clay brought forth.

Till the villain left the paths of ease
15 To walk in the perilous paths, and drive
The just man into barren climes.

Now the sneaking serpent walks
In mild humility,
And the just man rages in the wilds
20 Where lions roam.

Rintrah roars and shakes his fires in the burdened air;
Hungry clouds swag on the deep.

Plate 3

This is one of the most important passages in the *The Marriage of Heaven and Hell* and provides a key to the dialectic structure of the argument of **Songs of Innocence and of Experience**. Blake challenges the reader by inverting the meanings of some familiar ideas.

23   *a new heaven* – a new world.
        thirty-three years – Blake's age at the time of writing.

24   *the eternal hell* – the French Revolution, leading to good, but in the short term threatening the old order and the orthodox religions.

24   *Swedenborg* – Emanuel Swedenborg (1688–1772) was a scientist and mystic whose teaching led to a New Church of which Blake was a member; Blake subsequently rejected it because he increasingly detected the influence of Newtonian rationalism in Swedenborg's visionary writings.

25   *linen clothes* – the emptiness of Swedenborg's religious thought; Blake now saw him as a false prophet. (The reference is to *John*, 20,5-7.)

26   *Edom* – Esau, in the Bible, known for his revolutionary anger (*Genesis*, 32).

31   *religious* – the clergy.

> *What do you understand by the idea that progress depends on the notion of contraries?*

> *How do you interpret Blake's striking redefinition of good and evil?*

The Voice of the Devil
Plate 4

In order to promote some provocative, and indeed blasphemous views, Blake calls up a devil as his spokesman. Central to the devil's case is his advocacy of the role of energy (desire) and the consequences when it is restrained by reason. This in turn, the devil argues, leads to a passive response to authority. In order to clinch the argument, Blake's devil invokes Milton's *Paradise Lost*, where Satan is superficially a more attractive figure than God.

45-6   *the chief inlets of soul in this age* – the view of the eighteenth-century philosophers (e.g. Locke and Hartley) who believed that knowledge was acquired only through the senses, dismissing the rôle of the imagination.

Plate 3

As a new heaven is begun, and it is now thirty-three years since its
advent, the eternal hell revives. And lo! Swedenborg is the
25 angel sitting at the tomb; his writings are the linen clothes folded up.
Now is the dominion of Edom and the return of Adam into
Paradise (see Isaiah 34 and 35).

Without contraries is no progression. Attraction and
repulsion, reason and energy, love and hate, are necessary to
30 human existence.

From these contraries spring what the religious call good
and evil. Good is the passive that obeys reason. Evil is the
active springing from energy.

Good is heaven; evil is hell.

The Voice of the Devil
Plate 4

35 All Bibles or sacred codes have been the causes of the following
errors:

1. That man has two real existing principles, viz. a body and
a soul.

2. That energy, called evil, is alone from the body, and that
40 reason, called good, is alone from the soul.

3. That God will torment man in eternity for following his
energies.

But the following contraries to these are true:

1. Man has no body distinct from his soul, for that called
45 body is a portion of soul discerned by the five senses (the chief
inlets of soul in this age).

2. Energy is the only life and is from the body, and reason is
the bound or outward circumference of energy.

3. Energy is eternal delight.

Plates 5-6

56 *called* – i.e. by the religious.

70–71 *ratio of the five senses* – Milton's understanding of God was narrowly rational.
72 *fetters* – chains; (but figuratively) mind-forged manacles.

Why is it so important for Blake's argument for him to deny the dualism of body and soul?

What do you infer about the nature of the 'true poet'?

Plates 5-6

50   Those who restrain desire do so because theirs is weak
enough to be restrained; and the restrainer (or reason) usurps
its place and governs the unwilling.

And, being restrained, it by degrees becomes passive, till it
is only the shadow of desire.

55   The history of this is written in *Paradise Lost*, and the
governor (or reason) is called Messiah.

And the original archangel, or possessor of the command of
the heavenly host, is called the Devil, or Satan, and his children
are called Sin and Death.

60   But in the Book of Job, Milton's Messiah is called Satan.

For his history has been adopted by both parties.

It indeed appeared to Reason as if Desire was cast out. But
the Devil's account is that the Messiah fell, and formed a
heaven of what he stole from the abyss.

65   This is shown in the gospel, where he prays to the Father
to send the comforter, or Desire, that Reason may have ideas to
build on, the Jehovah of the Bible being no other than he who
dwells in flaming fire.

Know that after Christ's death he became Jehovah.

70   But in Milton the Father is destiny, the Son a ratio of the
five senses, and the Holy Ghost, vacuum!

Note: The reason Milton wrote in fetters when he wrote of
angels and God, and at liberty when of devils and hell, is
because he was a true poet and of the Devil's party without

75 knowing it.

A Memorable Fancy
Plates 6-7

Having established that hell is the source of wisdom and inspiration, Blake describes entering there to bring back 'some of their proverbs'.

85 *with corroding fires he wrote ...* – like Blake, engraving copper plates: 'printing in the infernal method, by corrosives which in hell are salutary and medicinal, melting surfaces away, and displaying the infinite which was hid' (see lines 244–47).

What do you think Blake understands by 'delighted with the enjoyments of genius' (lines 76–77)?

What do you understand by the sentence that the devil etches?

A Memorable Fancy
Plates 6-7

As I was walking among the fires of hell, delighted with the
enjoyments of genius (which to angels look like torment and
insanity), I collected some of their Proverbs, thinking that as
the sayings used in a nation mark its character, so the Proverbs
80 of Hell show the nature of infernal wisdom better than any
description of buildings or garments.

When I came home, on the abyss of the five senses, where a
flat-sided steep frowns over the present world, I saw a mighty
devil folded in black clouds, hovering on the sides of the rock.
85 With corroding fires he wrote the following sentence, now
perceived by the minds of men, and read by them on earth:

How do you know but ev'ry bird that cuts the airy way
Is an immense world of delight, closed by your senses five?

Proverbs of Hell
Plates 7-10

You should remember that the *Proverbs of Hell* are meant to satirize the received wisdom of the time. It is in their spirit, rather than their detail, that we should locate Blake's search for true wisdom.

103   *dearth* – shortage, famine.

122   *fell* – hide or skin.

Proverbs of Hell
Plates 7-10

In seed-time learn, in harvest teach, in winter enjoy.

90 Drive your cart and your plough over the bones of the dead.

The road to excess leads to the palace of wisdom.

Prudence is a rich ugly old maid courted by Incapacity.

He who desires but acts not breeds pestilence.

The cut worm forgives the plough.

95 Dip him in the river who loves water.

A fool sees not the same tree that a wise man sees.

He whose face gives no light shall never become a star.

Eternity is in love with the productions of time.

The busy bee has no time for sorrow.

100 The hours of folly are measured by the clock, but of wisdom no clock can measure.

All wholesome food is caught without a net or a trap.

Bring out number, weight and measure in a year of dearth.

No bird soars too high, if he soars with his own wings.

105 A dead body revenges not injuries.

The most sublime act is to set another before you.

If the fool would persist in his folly he would become wise.

Folly is the cloak of knavery.

Shame is pride's cloak.

110 Prisons are built with stones of Law, brothels with bricks of Religion.

The pride of the peacock is the glory of God.

The lust of the goat is the bounty of God.

The wrath of the lion is the wisdom of God.

115 The nakedness of woman is the work of God.

Excess of sorrow laughs; excess of joy weeps.

The roaring of lions, the howling of wolves, the raging of the stormy sea, and the destructive sword, are portions of eternity too great for the eye of man.

120 The fox condemns the trap, not himself.

Joys impregnate; sorrows bring forth.

Let man wear the fell of the lion, woman the fleece of the sheep.

142 *standing* – stagnant.

.

The bird a nest, the spider a web, man friendship.

The selfish, smiling fool and the sullen, frowning fool shall be
125   both thought wise, that they may be a rod.

What is now proved was once only imagined.

The rat, the mouse, the fox, the rabbit watch the roots; the lion, the
        tiger, the horse, the elephant, watch the fruits.

The cistern contains; the fountain overflows.
130   One thought fills immensity.

Always be ready to speak your mind, and a base man will avoid
        you.

Everything possible to be believed is an image of truth.

The eagle never lost so much time as when he submitted to learn
135   of the crow.

The fox provides for himself, but God provides for the lion.

Think in the morning, act in the noon, eat in the evening, sleep in
        the night.

He who has suffered you to impose on him knows you.
140   As the plough follows words, so God rewards prayers.

The tigers of wrath are wiser than the horses of instruction.

Expect poison from the standing water.

You never know what is enough, unless you know what is more
        than enough.
145   Listen to the fool's reproach! It is a kingly title!

The eyes of fire, the nostrils of air, the mouth of water, the beard
        of earth.

The weak in courage is strong in cunning.

The apple tree never asks the beech how he shall grow; nor the
150   lion the horse, how he shall take his prey.

The thankful receiver bears a plentiful harvest.

If others had not been foolish, we should be so.

The soul of sweet delight can never be defiled.

When thou seest an eagle, thou seest a portion of genius – lift up
155   thy head!

As the caterpillar chooses the fairest leaves to lay her eggs on, so
        the priest lays his curse on the fairest joys.

To create a little flower is the labour of ages.

'Damn!' braces; 'Bless!' relaxes.
160   The best wine is the oldest, the best water is the newest.

Prayers plough not; praises reap not.

Joys laugh not; sorrows weep not.

> Select a few of these proverbs that attract your attention and consider the implications of their meaning.

> How do you interpret the enigmatic line which concludes this extravagant and shocking series of proverbs?

Plate 11

This short, untitled plate furthers Blake's attack on the priesthood for promoting a rational religion which denies the divinity in the human.

> Why was the understanding of 'the ancient poets' superior to that of the contemporary priesthood?

> How does this piece develop the thinking in **Proverbs of Hell**?

The head sublime, the heart pathos, the genitals beauty, the
    hands and feet proportion.
165 As the air to a bird, or the sea to a fish, so is contempt to the
    contemptible.
The crow wished every thing was black; the owl, that every thing
    was white.
Exuberance is beauty.
170 If the lion was advised by the fox, he would be cunning.
Improvement makes straight roads, but the crooked roads
    without improvement are roads of genius.
Sooner murder an infant in its cradle than nurse unacted desires.
Where man is not, nature is barren.
175 Truth can never be told so as to be understood, and not be
    believed.
        Enough! Or too much.

Plate 11

The ancient poets animated all sensible objects with gods or
geniuses, calling them by the names and adorning them with
180 the properties of woods, rivers, mountains, lakes, cities,
nations, and whatever their enlarged and numerous senses
could perceive.
    And particularly they studied the genius of each city and
country, placing it under its mental deity.
185   Till a system was formed, which some took advantage of, and
enslaved the vulgar by attempting to realize or abstract the
mental deities from their objects: thus began priesthood;
    Choosing forms of worship from poetic tales.
    And at length they pronounced that the gods had ordered
190 such things.
    Thus men forgot that all deities reside in the human breast.

A Memorable Fancy
Plates 12-13

In these plates, Blake recounts dining with the the Old Testament prophets Isaiah and Ezekiel. Isaiah explodes the conventional idea that you can come to God through rational understanding. Ezekiel argues that true religion comes from the activity of the imagination, which confers on human beings a sense of the infinite.

What do you understand by the notion of 'poetic genius' here?

How does Ezekiel characterize the religion of Israel and its relationship to other religions?

A Memorable Fancy
Plates 12-13

The prophets Isaiah and Ezekiel dined with me, and I asked them
how they dared so roundly to assert that God spake to them,
and whether they did not think at the time that they would be
195   misunderstood, and so be the cause of imposition?

Isaiah answered, 'I saw no God, nor heard any, in a finite
organical perception. But my senses discovered the infinite in
everything, and, as I was then persuaded, and remain
confirmed, that the voice of honest indignation is the voice of
200   God, I cared not for consequences, but wrote.'

Then I asked, 'Does a firm persuasion that a thing is so,
make it so?'

He replied, 'All poets believe that it does, and in ages of
imagination this firm persuasion removed mountains; but many
205   are not capable of a firm persuasion of any thing.'

Then Ezekiel said, 'The philosophy of the east taught the first
principles of human perception. Some nations held one principle
for the origin and some another. We of Israel taught that the
poetic genius (as you now call it) was the first principle and all
210   the others merely derivative, which was the cause of our
despising the priests and philosophers of other countries, and
prophesying that all gods would at last be proved to originate in
ours and to be the tributaries of the poetic genius. It was this that
our great poet King David desired so fervently, and invokes so
215   pathetically, saying by this he conquers enemies and governs
kingdoms. And we so loved our God that we cursed in his name
all the deities of surrounding nations, and asserted that they had
rebelled. From these opinions the vulgar came to think that all
nations would at last be subject to the Jews.'

220   'This,' said he, 'like all firm persuasions, is come to pass, for
all nations believe the Jews' code and worship the Jews' God,
and what greater subjection can be?'

I heard this with some wonder, and must confess my own
conviction. After dinner I asked Isaiah to favour the world with
225   his lost works; he said none of equal value was lost. Ezekiel said
the same of his.

229   *Diogenes the Grecian* – a philosopher who, to demonstrate the
        virtues of austerity, took up residence in a large earthenware jar.

Plate 14

Here Blake envisages a breaking-up of the old ways of being and the
beginning of a new era based on the imagination and instincts instead of
reason.

237-238   *cherub ... tree of life* – in *Genesis*, the cherubim guarded the Tree of
        Knowledge after Adam and Eve were expelled from Eden.

245   *corrosives* – the acids used to etch copper plate.

248   *doors of perception* – the capacity of the imagination.

251   *chinks of his cavern* – the narrow understanding conferred by the five
       senses.

*Why does Blake describe the contribution his own engraving skills will make
to the new age as 'the infernal method'?*

*The final two lines of this plate contain Blake's own prophecy. What is his
vision and how is it expressed?*

I also asked of Isaiah what made him go naked and barefoot three years? He answered, 'The same that made our friend Diogenes, the Grecian.'

230   I then asked Ezekiel why he ate dung, and lay so long on his right and left side. He answered, 'The desire of raising other men into a perception of the infinite. This the North American tribes practise, and is he honest who resists his genius or conscience only for the sake of present ease or gratification?'

Plate 14

235   The ancient tradition that the world will be consumed in fire at the end of six thousand years is true, as I have heard from hell.

    For the cherub with his flaming sword is hereby commanded to leave his guard at the tree of life; and when he does, the whole creation will be consumed and appear infinite and holy,
240   whereas it now appears finite and corrupt.

    This will come to pass by an improvement of sensual enjoyment.

    But first the notion that man has a body distinct from his soul is to be expunged. This I shall do by printing in the infernal
245   method, by corrosives which in hell are salutary and medicinal, melting apparent surfaces away, and displaying the infinite which was hid.

    If the doors of perception were cleansed, everything would appear to man as it is: infinite.

250   For man has closed himself up till he sees all things through narrow chinks of his cavern.

A Memorable Fancy
Plate 15

This plate is an allegory of the ways in which the 'doors of perception' might be 'cleansed', and human beings freed from the intellectual constraints of the 'cavern'.

254 *dragon-man* – representing sensual pleasure, and rejecting conventional laws and morality.

257 *viper* – of reason.

260 *eagle* – of genius, which is capable of releasing creative faculties.

264 *lions of flaming fire* – true spirituality, which is the anger which burns hot enough to melt the metal, which is then cast by the 'unnamed forms', to make the books.

How do you account for the paradox of Blake including the viper of Reason in the process described here in the light of other things you have read?

How effective do you think this allegorical vision is?

A Memorable Fancy
Plate 15

I was in a printing-house in hell and I saw the method in which knowledge is transmitted from generation to generation.

255 In the first chamber was a dragon-man, clearing away the rubbish from a cave's mouth; within, a number of dragons were hollowing the cave.

In the second chamber was a viper folding round the rock and the cave, and others adorning it with gold, silver, and precious stones.

260 In the third chamber was an eagle with wings and feathers of air – he caused the insides of the cave to be infinite; around were numbers of eagle-like men, who built palaces in the immense cliffs.

In the fourth chamber were lions of flaming fire, raging around

265 and melting the metals into living fluids.

In the fifth chamber were unnamed forms, which cast the metals into the expanse.

There they were received by men who occupied the sixth chamber, and took the forms of books and were arranged in

270 libraries.

Plates 16-17

In these plates Blake divides humanity into those who have the God-like power of the creative imagination (the prolific) and those who are constrained by reason (the devourers).

271 *The giants* – the five senses, the sources of human energy.

293 *antediluvians* – the giants who existed before the Flood.

Why do you think Blake insists that the prolific and the devourers are natural enemies and cannot be reconciled?

Does the concluding image of Satan correspond with previous representations?

Plates 16-17

The giants who formed this world into its sensual existence and now seem to live in it in chains are, in truth, the causes of its life and the sources of all activity. But the chains are the cunning of weak and tame minds, which have power to resist energy.

275 According to the proverb, the weak in courage is strong in cunning.

Thus one portion of being is the prolific; the other, the devouring. To the devourer it seems as if the producer was in his chains, but it is not so: he only takes portions of existence
280 and fancies that the whole.

But the prolific would cease to be prolific unless the devourer, as a sea, received the excess of his delights.

Some will say: 'Is not God alone the prolific?' I answer, 'God only acts and is in existing beings or men.'

285 These two classes of men are always upon earth, and they should be enemies; whoever tries to reconcile them seeks to destroy existence.

Religion is an endeavour to reconcile the two.

Note: Jesus Christ did not wish to unite, but to separate
290 them (as in the parable of sheep and goats), and he says, 'I came not to send peace, but a sword.'

Messiah or Satan or Tempter was formerly thought to be one of the antediluvians who are our energies.

A Memorable Fancy
Plates 17-20

In this section Blake depicts himself arguing with an angel who speaks for conventional religion. The angel shows Blake the fate that awaits him if he continues to hold his radical views. Blake then responds in kind, and shows the angel his conception of eternity. Blake finally dismisses the angel as a time-waster. This is a detailed satire on orthodox religion and materialism.

301 *mill* – the angel's home, representing sterile rationalism or materialism.

313 *abyss* – for predestined souls (Blake totally rejected the idea of predestination which Swedenborg came to adopt).

316 *spiders* – good and evil powers: the space between them is purgatory.

A Memorable Fancy
Plates 17-20

An angel came to me and said, 'Oh, pitiable foolish young man!
Oh, horrible! Oh, dreadful state! Consider the hot burning
295 dungeon thou art preparing for thyself to all eternity, to which
thou art going in such career.'

I said, 'Perhaps you will be willing to show me my eternal
lot, and we will contemplate together upon it and see whether
your lot or mine is most desirable.'

300 So he took me through a stable, and through a church, and
down into the church-vault, at the end of which was a mill.
Through the mill we went, and came to a cave. Down the
winding cavern we groped our tedious way, till a void,
boundless as nether sky, appeared beneath us, and we held by
305 the roots of trees and hung over this immensity. But I said, 'If you
please, we will commit ourselves to this void, and see whether
providence is here also; if you will not, I will.' But he answered,
'Do not presume, oh young man; but as we here remain, behold
thy lot which will soon appear when the darkness passes away.'

310 So I remained with him, sitting in the twisted root of an oak.
He was suspended in a fungus which hung with the head
downward into the deep.

By degrees we beheld the infinite abyss, fiery as the smoke
of a burning city; beneath us, at an immense distance, was the
315 sun, black but shining; round it were fiery tracks on which
revolved vast spiders, crawling after their prey, which flew, or
rather swum, in the infinite deep, in the most terrific shapes of
animals sprung from corruption. And the air was full of them,
and seemed composed of them. These are devils, and are called
320 Powers of the Air. I now asked my companion which was my
eternal lot. He said, 'Between the black and white spiders.'

But now, from between the black and white spiders, a cloud
of fire burst and rolled through the deep, blackening all beneath,
so that the nether deep grew black as a sea, and rolled
325 with a terrible noise. Beneath us was nothing now to be seen but a
black tempest, till, looking east between the clouds and the waves,
we saw a cataract of blood mixed with fire; and not many stones'

333 *Leviathan* – the authority of Church and State which Thomas Hobbes
believed essential because of the natural sinfulness of human beings.

359 *the deep pit* – the Church of England.

362 *monkeys* – the devourers, those constrained by reason.

throw from us, appeared and sunk again the scaly fold of a
monstrous serpent. At last, to the east, distant about three
330 degrees, appeared a fiery crest above the waves. Slowly it reared,
like a ridge of golden rocks, till we discovered two globes of
crimson fire from which the sea fled away in clouds of smoke.
And now we saw it was the head of Leviathan. His forehead was
divided into streaks of green and purple, like those on a tiger's
335 forehead; soon we saw his mouth and red gills hang just above
the raging foam, tinging the black deep with beams of blood,
advancing towards us with all the fury of a spiritual existence.
    My friend the angel climbed up from his station into the
mill; I remained alone, and then this appearance was no more,
340 but I found myself sitting on a pleasant bank beside a river by
moonlight, hearing a harper who sung to the harp. And his
theme was, 'The man who never alters his opinion is like
standing water, and breeds reptiles of the mind.'
    But I arose and sought for the mill, and there I found my
345 angel, who, surprised, asked me how I escaped.
    I answered, 'All that we saw was owing to your metaphysics.
For when you ran away, I found myself on a bank by moonlight
hearing a harper. But now we have seen my eternal lot, shall I
show you yours?' He laughed at my proposal, but I by force
350 suddenly caught him in my arms, and flew westerly through the
night, till we were elevated above the earth's shadow. Then I
flung myself with him directly into the body of the sun; here I
clothed myself in white, and, taking in my hand Swedenborg's
volumes, sunk from the glorious clime, and passed all the
355 planets till we came to Saturn. Here I stayed to rest, and then
leaped into the void between Saturn and the fixed stars.
    'Here,' said I, 'is your lot – in this space (if space it may be
called).' Soon we saw the stable and the church, and I took him
to the altar, and opened the Bible, and lo! it was a deep pit, into
360 which I descended, driving the angel before me. Soon we saw
seven houses of brick. One we entered; in it were a number of
monkeys, baboons, and all of that species, chained by the
middle, grinning and snatching at one another, but withheld by
the shortness of their chains. However, I saw that they
365 sometimes grew numerous, and then the weak were caught by

373 *Aristotle's* Analytics – the logic of materialism.

The two visions of eternity in this section are in some ways mirror images. In what ways are they the same? How do they differ?

Explain what is meant by 'Opposition is true friendship'.

the strong, and, with a grinning aspect, first coupled with, and then devoured, by plucking off first one limb and then another, till the body was left a helpless trunk. This, after grinning and kissing it with seeming fondness, they devoured too. And here
370 and there I saw one savourily picking the flesh off his own tail. As the stench terribly annoyed us both, we went into the mill, and I in my hand brought the skeleton of a body, which in the mill was Aristotle's *Analytics*.

So the angel said, 'Thy fantasy has imposed upon me, and
375 thou oughtest to be ashamed.'

I answered, 'We impose on one another, and it is but lost time to converse with you whose works are only analytics.'

Opposition is true friendship.

This is a plain-speaking attack on Swedenborg.

400 *Paracelsus or Jacob Behmen [Boehme]* – mystic writers widely read in Blake's time; both emphasized the role of the imagination in arriving at a sense of spiritual truth – further evidence of the 'divine' in humanity.

How effective do you find the final image?

On what grounds does Blake criticize Swedenborg?

Plates 21-22

I have always found that angels have the vanity to speak of
380 themselves as the only wise; this they do with a confident
insolence sprouting from systematic reasoning.

Thus Swedenborg boasts that what he writes is new, though
it is only the contents or index of already published books.

A man carried a monkey about for a show, and, because he
385 was a little wiser than the monkey, grew vain, and conceived
himself as much wiser than seven men. It is so with
Swedenborg: he shows the folly of churches, and exposes
hypocrites, till he imagines that all are religious, and himself
the single one on earth that ever broke a net.

390 Now hear the plain fact: Swedenborg has not written one
new truth. Now hear another: he has written all the old
falsehoods.

And now hear the reason: he conversed with angels who are
all religious, and conversed not with devils who all hate religion,
395 for he was incapable through his conceited notions.

Thus Swedenborg's writings are a recapitulation of all
superficial opinions, and an analysis of the more sublime – but
no further.

Have now another plain fact: any man of mechanical talents
400 may, from the writings of Paracelsus or Jacob Behmen, produce
ten thousand volumes of equal value with Swedenborg's –
and, from those of Dante or Shakespeare, an infinite number.

But when he has done this, let him not say that he knows
better than his master, for he only holds a candle in sunshine.

A Memorable Fancy
Plates 23-24

Blake returns to the theme of divinity in humanity expressed through creativity, imagination and impulse. So strong is the case that Blake (here as a devil) builds, that he converts an angel to his point of view. The *Fancy* concludes with the symbolic marriage of heaven and hell.

418   *Bray* – beat, pound.

433   *flame of fire* – passion, indignation, revolution – appropriate to a conversion.

434   *Elijah* – the Old Testament prophet who communicated directly with God, and who was carried to heaven in a fiery chariot.

438   *Bible of hell* – Blake's writings, actual and planned.

Why, in the devil's opinion, is Jesus 'the greatest man'?

What do you understand by the last sentence?

A Memorable Fancy
Plates 23-24

405   Once I saw a devil in a flame of fire, who arose before a
     that sat on a cloud, and the devil uttered these words:
       'The worship of God is honouring his gifts in other men, each
     according to his genius, and loving the greatest men best. Those
     who envy or calumniate great men hate God, for there is no
410   other God.'
       The angel hearing this became almost blue; but, mastering
     himself, he grew yellow, and, at last, white, pink and smiling.
     And then replied:
       'Thou idolater! Is not God one? And is not he visible in Jesus
415   Christ? And has not Jesus Christ given his sanction to the law of
     ten commandments, and are not all other men fools, sinners, and
     nothings?'
       The devil answered, 'Bray a fool in a mortar with wheat, yet
     shall not his folly be beaten out of him. If Jesus Christ is the
420   greatest man, you ought to love him in the greatest degree; now
     hear how he has given his sanction to the law of ten
     commandments. Did he not mock at the Sabbath, and so mock
     the Sabbath's God? Murder those who were murdered because
     of him? Turn away the law from the woman taken in adultery?
425   Steal the labour of others to support him? Bear false witness when
     he omitted making a defence before Pilate? Covet when he
     prayed for his disciples, and when he bid them shake off the
     dust of their feet against such as refused to lodge them? I tell
     you, no virtue can exist without breaking these ten
430   commandments: Jesus was all virtue, and acted from impulse –
     not from rules.'
       When he had so spoken, I beheld the angel who stretched
     out his arms embracing the flame of fire, and he was consumed
     and arose as Elijah.
435   Note: This angel, who is now become a devil, is my particular
     friend. We often read the Bible together in its infernal or
     diabolical sense, which the world shall have if they behave well.
       I have also the Bible of hell, which the world shall have
     whether they will or no.
440   One law for the lion and ox is oppression.

A Song of Liberty
Plates 25-27

These final plates explore the significance of, and celebrate, the French and American Revolutions as representing a move towards the liberation of humanity from the tyranny of Church and State.

441   *The Eternal Female groaned* – apprehension at the social and political upheavals.

442   *Albion* – England.

444   *rend down thy dungeon* – the fall of the Bastille, 14 July 1789.

445   *Rome* – the Roman Catholic Church.

449   *the new-born terror* – the spirit of revolution.

451   *the new-born fire stood before the starry king* – the newly-conceived French Republic repelled an invasion from Austria and Prussia in 1792.

452   *Flagged* – hampered.

466   *the jealous king* – his fall represents the success of the American Revolution.

470   *Urthona* – imagination, the most important quality released by the collapse of tyranny.

A Song of Liberty
Plates 25-27

1. The Eternal Female groaned! It was heard over all the earth:

2. Albion's coast is sick, silent; the American meadows faint!

3. Shadows of prophecy shiver along by the lakes and the rivers, and mutter across the ocean! France, rend down thy dungeon!

445   4. Golden Spain, burst the barriers of old Rome!

5. Cast thy keys, oh Rome, into the deep, down falling, even to eternity down falling,

6. And weep!

7. In her trembling hands, she took the new-born terror howling;

450   8. On those infinite mountains of light now barred out by the Atlantic sea, the new-born fire stood before the starry king!

9. Flagged with grey-browed snows and thunderous visages, the jealous wings waved over the deep.

10. The speary hand burned aloft, unbuckled was the shield, forth

455   went the hand of jealousy among the flaming hair, and hurled the new-born wonder through the starry night.

11. The fire, the fire, is falling!

12. Look up! Look up! Oh citizen of London, enlarge thy countenance! Oh Jew, leave counting gold, return to thy oil and

460   wine! Oh African, black African! (Go, winged thought, widen his forehead.)

13. The fiery limbs, the flaming hair, shot like the sinking sun into the western sea.

14. Waked from his eternal sleep, the hoary element roaring fled

465   away;

15. Down rushed, beating his wings in vain, the jealous king; his grey-browed counsellors, thunderous warriors, curled veterans, among helms and shields and chariots, horses, elephants, banners, castles, slings and rocks,

470   16. Falling, rushing, ruining! – buried in the ruins, on Urthona's dens.

17. All night beneath the ruins; then, their sullen flames faded, emerge round the gloomy king.

474 *starry hosts* – the Newtonian universe, limiting imagination.

477 *son of fire in his eastern cloud* – French republicanism.

481 *Empire is no more!* – looks back to the American Revolution, celebrates the French Revolution and looks forward to the end of the Spanish and Papal empires.

482 *the raven of dawn* – the fear of death.

485 *nor pale religious lechery call that virginity that wishes but acts not* – hypocrisy.

What is the significance of Blake's appeal to a 'citizen of London' in line 458?

What do you understand by the final words of this plate?

18. With thunder and fire, leading his starry hosts through the
475 waste wilderness, he promulgates his ten commands, glancing his
beamy eyelids over the deep in dark dismay,
19. Where the son of fire in his eastern cloud, while the morning
plumes her golden breast,
20. Spurning the clouds written with curses, stamps the stony law
480 to dust, loosing the eternal horses from the dens of night, crying,

'Empire is no more! And now the lion and wolf shall cease.'

Chorus

Let the priests of the raven of dawn no longer, in deadly black, with
hoarse note, curse the sons of joy; nor his accepted brethren
(whom, tyrant, he calls free) lay the bound or build the roof;
485 nor pale religious lechery call that virginity that wishes but acts not.
For everything that lives is holy.

Other Poems and Extracts

And did those feet in ancient time

This poem opens with Blake's vision of an England before it was corrupted by progress and rationalism in its various forms, and goes on to be a rousing call for renewal.

1   *those feet* – not the feet of Christ but those of Joseph of Arimathea, considered by Blake and others to be the founder of English Christianity.

5   *countenance divine* – God.

7   *Jerusalem* – the Holy City of Peace, which is the perfect society and the divine vision in all individuals.

9-12   Blake's call to arms is primarily intellectual, but some commentators have found a sexual allusion here.

12   *chariot of fire* – the Old Testament prophet Elijah ascended to heaven in a chariot of fire.

It would be easy to interpret the 'dark satanic mills' as the factories and cotton mills of the Industrial Revolution. In the light of your reading of other works by Blake criticizing English society, what else might the phrase suggest?

What does Blake offer as an antidote to the situation that the poem describes? In what way does the structure contribute towards this?

Other Poems and Extracts

And did those feet in ancient time

And did those feet in ancient time
Walk upon England's mountains green?
And was the holy lamb of God
On England's pleasant pastures seen?

5 And did the countenance divine
Shine forth upon our clouded hills?
And was Jerusalem builded here,
Among these dark satanic mills?

Bring me my bow of burning gold!
10 Bring me my arrows of desire!
Bring me my spear – oh clouds, unfold!
Bring me my chariot of fire!

I will not cease from mental fight
Nor shall my sword sleep in my hand,
15 Till we have built Jerusalem
In England's green and pleasant land.

From *Auguries of Innocence*

In parts of this poem Blake articulates characteristics of his ways of seeing. In the body of the poem he demonstrates through a series of mainly unrelated couplets his understanding of those social ills and attitudes of mind to which his vision gives him access.

From *Auguries of Innocence*

To see a world in a grain of sand
And heaven in a wild flower,
Hold infinity in the palm of your hand
And eternity in an hour.

5   A robin redbreast in a cage
Puts all heaven in a rage.
A dove house filled with doves and pigeons
Shudders hell through all its regions.
A dog starved at his master's gate
10 Predicts the ruin of the state.
A horse misused upon the road
Calls to heaven for human blood.
Each outcry of the hunted hare
A fibre from the brain does tear.
15 A skylark wounded in the wing,
A cherubim does cease to sing.
The gamecock clipped and armed for fight
Does the rising sun affright.
Every wolf's and lion's howl
20 Raises from hell a human soul.
The wild deer, wand'ring here and there,
Keeps the human soul from care.
The lamb misused breeds public strife
And yet forgives the butcher's knife.
[...]
25 It is right it should be so;
Man was made for joy and woe;
And when this we rightly know
Through the world we safely go.
Joy and woe are woven fine,
30 A clothing for the soul divine.
Under every grief and pine
Runs a joy with silken twine.
[...]

34   *palsied* – paralysed.

37   *mite* – a small coin of low value.

47   *emmet* – ant.

58   *winding sheet* – cloth used to cover a corpse.

The soldier, armed with sword and gun,
Palsied strikes the summer's sun.
35 The poor man's farthing is worth more
Than all the gold on Afric's shore.
One mite wrung from the labourer's hands
Shall buy and sell the miser's lands;
Or, if protected from on high,
40 Does that whole nation sell and buy.
He who mocks the infant's faith
Shall be mocked in age and death.
He who shall teach the child to doubt,
The rotting grave shall ne'er get out.
45 He who respects the infant's faith
Triumphs over hell and death.
[...]
The emmet's inch and eagle's mile
Make lame philosophy to smile.
He who doubts from what he sees
50 Will ne'er believe, do what you please.
If the sun and moon should doubt,
They'd immediately go out.
To be in a passion you good may do,
But no good if a passion is in you.
55 The whore and gambler, by the state
Licensed, build that nation's fate.
The harlot's cry from street to street
Shall weave old England's winding sheet.
The winner's shout, the loser's curse,
60 Dance before dead England's hearse.
Every night and every morn
Some to misery are born.
Every morn and every night
Some are born to sweet delight.
65 Some are born to sweet delight,
Some are born to endless night.

What aspects of Blake's ways of seeing are highlighted in this poem?

By what means does Blake assert the unity of the cosmos in this poem?

How would you resolve the paradox of Blake, who was well-known as a dissenter, attacking the mischief caused by doubt and scepticism? Look particularly at lines 41–52.

Why should I care for the men of Thames

It is interesting to compare this poem, thought to be have been written before 1794, with London in **Songs of Experience**.

7 *Ohio* – a river which flows into the Mississippi; a reference to the American Revolution.

8 *I was born a slave, but I go to be free* – compare 'Man is born free; and everywhere he is in chains' (Rousseau, **The Social Contract**, 1762).

How successful is this poem when compared with London?

The final line may conflict with ideas expressed in later poems. What different views does Blake offer in Infant Joy and Infant Sorrow in **Songs of Innocence and of Experience**?

We are led to believe a lie
When we see not through the eye,
Which was born in a night to perish in a night
70   When the soul slept in beams of light.
God appears and God is light
To those poor souls who dwell in night.
But does a human form display
To those who dwell in realms of day.

Why should I care for the men of Thames

Why should I care for the men of Thames,
Or the cheating waves of chartered streams;
Or shrink at the little blasts of fear
That the hireling blows into my ear?

5   Though born on the cheating banks of Thames,
Though his waters bathed my infant limbs,
The Ohio shall wash his stains from me:
I was born a slave, but I go to be free!

BACKGROUND

William Blake, Author and Illustrator

Throughout his life, William Blake (1757–1827) was a radical and vision-
ary, and these two aspects of his genius must be seen as interdependent.
His radicalism – political, religious and artistic – was in part shaped by
his background and upbringing. What gave it a distinctive quality, how-
ever, was Blake's astonishingly vivid imagination – so vivid, in fact, that
the world around him was in some ways less real than his visions. This
visionary capacity, of course, helped to fuel the charge made by his
detractors that he was insane. In fact, it endowed Blake with a creative
freedom in his poetry, engravings and paintings to express the truth as
he saw it and to promote social and political change through an imagi-
native transformation of the world.

He was born in London in 1757. His parents were hosiers – stocking
weavers – and while that was a respectable occupation, it was no guar-
antee of luxury or comfort for William and his three brothers. Through-
out his life, Blake was never financially secure and he had to work for
his living as an engraver and publisher in addition to illustrating his own
work. His genius was largely unrecognized in his own time and he also
suffered a series of commercial disasters which meant that poverty was
never very far away. In 1782 he married Catherine Boucher, the illiterate
daughter of a market gardener. The couple remained childless. When
Blake died in 1827 he was without debts but he was buried in an un-
marked grave.

Blake was initially educated at home, largely by his mother, and this
experience instilled from the start an independence of mind. When he
was ten he went to a drawing school, and at the age of fourteen he was
apprenticed as an engraver. In 1779, in his early twenties, he studied at
the Royal Academy but was later to reject its traditional approach to art
and in particular the ideas of its President, Sir Joshua Reynolds.
Reynolds believed that artists should imitate the past masters and seek
commissions from wealthy patrons. Blake felt that this approach not
only neglected the inspiration of genius but, worse, implied that artistic
creation was an entirely rational process. His own mental life suggested
quite the contrary.

From his earliest years, Blake was a visionary, subject to vivid 'waking' dreams and terrifying nightmares. When he was four years old he said that God had appeared to him at the window and on another occasion he claimed to have seen a tree full of angels. Once he rushed home to tell his surprised mother that he had seen the prophet Ezekiel sitting under a tree. How should we understand these claims? In part they may suggest a (not uncommon) refuge from the unhappiness of childhood. More significantly, we can perhaps already detect a kind of moral protest by a sensitive child against the harsh reality of late eighteenth-century society, and indeed of the human condition, which was to inform his later writing. It was early evidence of that imaginative capacity to transform the real world that was to be seen in *Songs of Innocence*. And just as there, where the ideal dream world is threatened by the evil and corruption described in *Songs of Experience*, so the young Blake's optimistic 'waking' visions were overwhelmed by darker fears and anxieties when he slept and he was tortured by nightmares. The positive and negative images which haunted his imagination in these years were to resurface later – and to inform the patterns of symbolism in the poetry.

Blake's social and political radicalism, however distinctive its manner of expression, was to an extent influenced by his parents. They were religious dissenters and this puts his background firmly in a tradition of hostility towards the Church of England and, inevitably at this time, the State. Coming from humble origins himself, his sympathies were always with the common people and he hated the inequities perpetrated by the still powerful eighteenth-century alliance of monarchy, aristocracy and Church. Blake rejoiced that the old order was being challenged and later gave his enthusiastic support to the French and American Revolutions. However, while he belonged to the dissenting tradition, he was often at odds with the dissenting sects and the radical political groups who might have been seen as his natural allies. As a consequence, he was never part of a mainstream anti-establishment movement, but was rather a single voice, striving to be heard above the clamour of late eighteenth-century political and religious life.

To some extent this can be explained by the fact that Blake was a radical in more than simply political terms. Indeed, he was opposed to the very ways of thinking in his age. The philosophers and scientists of the eighteenth century had promoted a rationalist and materialist world view which was to prove very influential and has survived into the twentieth century. Blake traced this process back to Isaac Newton (1642–1727) whose classical physics had generated a view of the universe as a great clockwork machine, all the laws of which we would eventually come to know. Blake hated this kind of understanding, feeling that it was anti-human and took all the mystery out of God's creation. Blake might sympathize with the dissenters' and radicals' opposition to the old order of Church and King, but he rejected their faith in rationalism as the only basis for a *new* social and political order. His own mental experience suggested that there were other, more imaginative, ways of seeing, and more importantly, other forms of truth.

Consequently, Blake sought to write in quite new and challenging ways in order to offer an antidote to those habits of mind which were shaping the emergent social, political and religious conditions of the period. His poetry demonstrated a new and distinctive voice and this is evident in *Songs of Innocence and of Experience* and in the later Prophetic Books, e.g. *Europe: A Prophecy*, *The Book of Urizen* and *The Four Zoas*. Above all, then, Blake thought that art should be politically committed and continually challenge the dominant ideologies of the day.

Thus Blake's visionary capacities, and the symbolism derived from the dreams and nightmares of his childhood, shaped a philosophy and a language which were opposed to the scientific and materialist tendencies of his age. In celebrating the creative power of the imagination he wished to demonstrate ways of seeing which went beyond the understanding of the scientists and had the potential to improve the human lot. An inspired – and prophetic – art should, in Blake's view, be enlisted in the service of humanity. In this way his radicalism and his poetic vision can be seen to be complementary. His was in every sense a revolutionary art.

Social and Political Background

Introduction

One way of establishing the importance of William Blake is to understand that he was writing at a time when our modern world was born. The literary, artistic and cultural movement known as Romanticism – in which Blake is perhaps one of the first major figures – emerged at the same time as far-reaching changes were taking place in all areas of British life.

The key word is 'revolution' – both at home and abroad. The Industrial Revolution initiated remarkable changes in manufacture and production based on technological and scientific developments. It created new wealth for the commercial and professional middle classes who increasingly challenged the power base of the landed gentry and their allies in the Established Church (the rise of dissent, and especially Methodism, is an important factor here). And it called into being an exploited industrial underclass who did not share in the new wealth.

The Agrarian Revolution was prompted by an urgent need to feed an exploding population. The Enclosure Acts meant that common land passed into private ownership and, with developments in agricultural science, became productive arable land – but in the short term this brought hardship with the decline of subsistence farming and the loss of grazing rights. Starving country people were increasingly forced into the squalid slums of the growing manufacturing towns. Thus in a context of the rise of capitalism, shifting power structures and increasing social unrest, modern Britain was born: urban, industrial, democratic, secular and religiously plural.

These transformations in British social, political and economic life were accelerated by developments abroad. It is sometimes said that the American Revolution had as great an impact on this side of the Atlantic as it did in the Thirteen Colonies: it changed the political and social complexion of Britain. The Declaration of Independence announced a break with older hierarchical social structures and in particular the petty tyranny of George III:

> We hold these truths to be self-evident, that all men are created equal, that they are endowed by their Creator with certain inalienable Rights, that among these are Life, Liberty, and the Pursuit of Happiness – That

to secure these rights, Governments are instituted among Men, deriv-
ing their just powers from the consent of the governed.

Monarchical and aristocratic government – and the politics of deference
– were fatally undermined in Britain, and great impetus was given to the
growing call for democracy and parliamentary reform. Blake, who hated
George III, was a whole-hearted supporter of the American Revolution.

There were even more startling developments across the Channel.
Some thinkers saw the French Revolution as bringing about the 'end of
history', in other words a new beginning for human society where the
ancien régime (based on the privileges of nobility and king) would be
overthrown and liberty, equality and fraternity would prevail. In Amer-
ica and France, the radical political thinking of the eighteenth-century
Enlightenment with its emphasis on the perfectibility of man and the
attainment of general happiness in a society constructed on a more ra-
tional basis, seemed to be taking shape in the real world.

This optimism was short-lived. The French Revolution collapsed into
internecine violence with the Reign of Terror in 1793–4. For those who
had placed so many hopes in the Revolution – and this included Blake,
and the other Romantic poets such as Wordsworth and Coleridge –
worse was to follow when France, ostensibly to spread the Revolution
abroad, began under the leadership of Napoleon to invade other Euro-
pean countries in a bid for European dominance which was to last for
twenty years. This seemed to be the final betrayal of the high ideals of
the Revolution. Blake's disillusionment with the course of the Revolu-
tion is reflected in the darker mood of *Songs of Experience*.

In Britain, initial sympathy for the Revolution soon began to wane as
power in France passed into the hands of the extremists. The atrocities
associated with the Reign of Terror enhanced this conservative reaction
which was confirmed by the execution of Louis XVI. In 1793, France
declared war on Britain. This had serious consequences for the British
economy and much hardship ensued for the poor during the years to
1815. This was made worse by a series of poor harvests and the on-going
consequences of industrialization and urbanization. In the absence of
any significant intervention by the government to alleviate the situation,
there was an upsurge in radical thought and activity (including rioting
and violence) which the government – in a panic about the French Revo-
lution and fearing an invasion – took firm steps to repress. During this
period of deepening social crisis, Blake's sympathies were always with

the sufferings of ordinary people. The climate of the period is, however, reflected in the fact that he was himself accused of sedition (but subsequently acquitted) in 1803.

A revolutionary era ended with the defeat of Napoleon and the restoration of the Bourbons. Other European monarchies, whose future had looked bleak, were re-established and the Congress of Vienna went a long way towards restoring the *status quo* on the continent. Nevertheless, the revolutionary spirit lived on and social and political thinking was changed irrevocably.

CHRONOLOGICAL TABLE

1757	William Blake born
1760	George III becomes King
1762	Jean-Jacques Rousseau publishes *The Social Contract*
1763	Hargreaves' spinning jenny
1765	Rioting in London
1769	James Watts' steam engine
	Richard Arkwright's water-powered spinning frame
1773	Darby's cast-iron bridge
1775	American War of Independence begins (Declaration of Independence, 1776)
1776	Adam Smith publishes *The Wealth of Nations*
1780	Anti-Catholic Gordon Riots (witnessed by Edmund Burke)
1783	Treaty of Paris establishes American independence
1789	Fall of Bastille initiates the French Revolution (Declaration of the Rights of Man)
	Louis XVI and family seized at Versailles and forced to return to Paris
	Blake publishes *Songs of Innocence*
1790	Louis XVI proclaimed constitutional monarch in France
	Edmund Burke publishes *Reflections on the Revolution in France*
1791	Flight and recapture of Louis XVI
	'Church and King' mob sack home of radical philosopher Joseph Priestley in Birmingham
	Blake publishes *The French Revolution*
	Thomas Paine publishes *The Rights of Man Part I*
1792	France declared a republic, repels invasion from Austria and Prussia
	Increasingly bitter rivalry between Jacobins (extreme Republicans, clerks and artisans of Paris) and Girondins (middle-class, moderate idealistic Republicans who were initially in control of the Legislative Assembly)
1793	Girondins lose initiative
	Execution of Louis XVI and Marie Antoinette
	France declares war on Britain
	Reign of Terror (to 1794) led by Robespierre and Jacobins: mass executions (40,000 guillotined) in Paris and other cities of 'enemies of the people'
	Execution of the Girondins
	Blake publishes *The Marriage of Heaven and Hell, Visions of the Daughters of Albion* and *America: a Prophecy*
	William Godwin publishes *An Enquiry concerning Political Justice*
1794	Jacobins turn on each other: execution of Danton, fall of Robespierre
	Habeas Corpus Act suspended in Britain
	Blake publishes *Songs of Experience, Songs of Innocence and of Experience: Showing the Two Contrary States of the Human Soul* and *Europe: a Prophecy*

1795	France conquers the Netherlands and the Rhineland
	The Two Acts ban seditious meetings and treasonable
	conspiracy in Britain
1796	Napoleon's campaign in Italy; fears that France, now dominant
	in Europe, will invade Britain
1797	Naval mutinies at The Nore and Spithead leave Britain vulnerable
	to the French
	Insurrection in Ireland
	French seize Venice and Treaty of Campio Formio abolished
	Venetian Republic
1798	Irish rebellion crushed
	Napoleon invades Switzerland
	France invades Egypt but French fleet destroyed at Battle of the Nile
	Wordsworth and Coleridge publish the first edition of *Lyrical Ballads*
	Thomas Malthus publishes *Essay on the Principles of Population*
1799	Napoleon becomes First Consul following military coup in France
1800	Population 10.5 million
1802	Peace of Amiens (truce with French)
1803	War with France resumed
1804	Napoleon proclaimed Emperor
	Blake publishes revised version of *The Four Zoas*
1805	Battle of Trafalgar
1807	Abolition of slave trade
	France invades Spain and Portugal
1808	Blake publishes final version of *Milton*
1809	Following British intervention, the Convention of Cintra allows
	French to withdraw from Portugal
	Duke of Wellington starts campaign against French in Spain
1810	Economic depression in Britain as Napoleon enforces European trade
	blockade
1811	George III insane and Prince of Wales becomes Regent
1812	Luddites (machine breakers) attack textile frames and factories
	Napoleon invades Russia (retreat from Moscow)
1813	Wellington liberates Spain
	French withdraw from Holland, Italy and Switzerland
1814	Fall of Paris as allied armies invade France
	Napoleon abdicates and flees to Elba
	Congress of Vienna
	Stephenson's *Rocket*
1815	Napoleon returns from exile but is defeated at the Battle of Waterloo
1816	Economic depression in Britain
1817	Habeas Corpus Act again suspended
1819	Peterloo Massacre, Manchester (11 killed and perhaps 600 injured)
	The Six Acts prohibit radical activity
1820	Death of George III and accession of George IV
	Blake completes *Jerusalem: the Emanation of the Giant Albion*
1827	Blake dies

Cultural and Literary Background

Introduction

The term Romanticism describes a profound change of sensibility – of ways of thought and feeling – that took place in Europe at the end of the eighteenth and beginning of the nineteenth centuries. Related developments in literature, political thought, philosophy and religion all contributed to the emergence of a movement of which the influence continues to be felt at the end of the twentieth century. Current ideas about the individual, society, nature and art – and the relationships between them – all owe something to the Romantic movement. And the poetry, paintings and etchings of William Blake made a major contribution to this revolution in ways of seeing.

Again, 'revolution' is a key word. Romanticism in part drew its impetus from the political revolutions in America and France. To begin with, at least, it espoused the cause of liberty, of democracy and the rights of man, and in this respect it endorsed eighteenth-century Enlightenment thinking. But Romanticism should also be seen as a reaction against the scientific and rationalist philosophies of the Enlightenment, haunted as they were by Isaac Newton and Classical Physics. These philosophies not only seemed to have gone some way towards erasing God, or at least 'mystery', from the universe, but also provided the impetus for the transformation of Britain into an industrial and urban culture. A basic paradox to grasp, then, is that the Romantic writers were both of their times and opposed to them. Blake was typical in this dual response: he subscribed to the politics of the Enlightenment, but not to what he saw as the 'single vision' of Newtonian materialism.

Therefore, although the ideological foundations of Romanticism may be confused – and indeed became increasingly contradictory – certain concepts were at its core and found their most significant expression in a new kind of literature:

- liberty (the equivalent at a personal level of the political revolutions taking place in America and France)
- the primacy of authentic individual experience (the 'self')
- an emphasis on intense feeling (including terror)
- the creative imagination (for Blake, the God-like power in humanity)

- the importance of nature (as a source of vital power and as a moral guide)

Developments in a number of fields and some influential texts should be noted in the formation of these ideas.

Literature

The literature of Romanticism comprised a reaction against the so-called 'Augustan' writers earlier in the eighteenth century, such as Alexander Pope, Jonathan Swift and Samuel Johnson, whose themes and style were shaped by the Enlightenment. A famous poem by Samuel Johnson starts like this:

> Let observation with extensive view,
> Survey mankind, from China to Peru;
> Remark each anxious toil, each eager strife,
> And watch the busy scenes of crowded life;
> Then say how hope and fear, desire and hate,
> O'erspread with snares the clouded maze of fate,
> Where wav'ring man, betray'd by vent'rous pride,
> To tread the dreary paths without a guide;
> As treach'rous phantoms in the mist delude,
> Shuns fancied ills, or chases airy good.
> How rarely reason guides the stubborn choice,
> Rules the bold hand, or prompts the suppliant voice,
> How nations sink, by darling schemes oppress'd,
> When vengeance listens to the fool's request.
>
> *The Vanity of Human Wishes* (1749)

It is worthwhile considering the ways in which writing like this differs from that of the Romantics and of William Blake in particular. Adopting a tone of lofty detachment and moral seriousness, Johnson sets out to reveal the varieties of human folly when pride and ambition triumph over reason, restraint and moderation ('How rarely reason guides the stubborn choice'). This was characteristic of the Augustans. Their concern was with the behaviour of men and women in society ('the busy scenes of crowded life') and the rules of moral conduct. Consequently, satire was their favourite mode – a literary means of exposing and attacking 'vent'rous pride' and human egotism.

The agenda of the Romantic writers was to be quite different. Instead of reason, they celebrated emotion. Indeed, they wished to put mystery, and the irrational, back into a universe they felt to have been devalued by a mechanistic Newtonian world view. Instead of rules, they celebrated freedom in life and art. Where the Augustans put the emphasis on humans as social beings, the Romantics celebrated the individual. For the Augustans, nature was human nature (seen largely in urban settings) whereas for the Romantics it denoted the countryside as a source of inspiration and moral guidance (although this is probably less true of Blake than, say, William Wordsworth). For the Augustans, the imagination – which for Blake was the God-like power in human beings and the fount of wisdom and insight – was a source of delusion (the 'treach'rous phantoms' in Johnson's poem). Unlike the Romantics, therefore, self-expression, and the exploration of new areas of experience, were not priorities for these writers. On the contrary, they concentrated on expressing what they saw as timeless and universal truths – 'What oft was thought, but ne'er so well expressed' as Pope put it in *An Essay on Man*.

In the light of Pope's remark, it is clear that the Augustans placed great emphasis on the craftsmanship of the poet. The skill of the writer lay in the successful manipulation of existing poetic forms (usually the heroic couplet, as in *The Vanity of Human Wishes*) to communicate the theme. This explains the vogue for imitation by the Augustan writers of past masters of the art (*The Vanity of Human Wishes* is an imitation of the *Tenth Satire* of the Roman writer Juvenal). The pleasure for a sophisticated reader derived from the perception of how the writer had exploited figurative language and the couplet form to 'dress up' a thought. By contrast, the Romantics were much more experimental in finding ways of expressing their authentic feelings and developed the notion of 'organic form'. By this they meant that the form of a poem was to be dictated by the emotion, the subject and treatment, and not by pre-existing conventions. This accounts for Blake's deliberately simple, even childlike, style in *Songs of Innocence* – and it is also a conscious reaction to writing like that of Johnson.

Thus, the Romantic writers switched attention from subject, form and audience, which were uppermost for the Augustans, to the poet's own mind, feelings and ideas. Inspiration and genius were valued above decorum and the poet assumed the role of prophet and visionary.

This is especially true of William Blake. But it would be a mistake to assume that he appeared out of the blue. From the mid-eighteenth century the emergence of the Romantic sensibility, which his work so confidently expressed, was evinced by the appearance of new themes and emphases in both poetry and fiction.

- Descriptions of natural scenes and meditative style; nature as moral teacher
  William Cowper: *The Task* (1785)
  William Lisle Bowles: *Fourteen Sonnets* (1789)
  James Thomson: *The Seasons* (1726-30)

- Medieval past, the ballad form and the figure of the hero
  Bishop Percy: *Reliques of Early English Poetry* (1764)

- The cult of the primitive
  William Collins: *Ode on Popular Superstitions of the Highlands* (1788)
  Macpherson's Ossianic poetry

- The inspired poet as social prophet/visionary in a sublime and savage landscape
  Thomas Gray: *The Bard* (1757)

- Solitary meditations on the human condition
  Thomas Gray: *Elegy Written in a Country Churchyard* (1751)
  Edward Young: *The Complaint or Night Thoughts on Life, Death and Immortality* (1742-5)

- Foregrounding of those on the margins of society – the rural poor, children, servants, the criminal, the insane and women
  Henry Fielding: *Joseph Andrews* (1742)
  Samuel Richardson: *Pamela* (1739); and *Clarissa* (1748)

- Gothic horror, the terrors of the imagination and the supernatural, dreams and fairy tales
  Horace Walpole: *The Castle of Otranto* (1765).

The coming of age of this new literary movement was confirmed by the publication of Blake's *Songs of Innocence and of Experience* in 1794 and Wordsworth and Coleridge's *Lyrical Ballads* in 1797-8. In fiction, the vogue for the Gothic novel reached its height with Ann Radcliffe's *The Mysteries of Udolpho* (1794), and M. G. Lewis' *The Monk* (1796).

Politics

The two most influential writers here are Edmund Burke (1729-97) and Thomas Paine (1737-1809) whose writings highlight the fundamental ideological divisions of the period and the contradictions at the heart of Romanticism itself.

Edmund Burke: *Reflections on the Revolution in France* (1790)

This was an assault on the ideas which had inspired the Revolution. Burke rejected the idea that reason could bring about a complete break with the past (i.e. the 'end of history') and thereby fashion an ideal society. He considered the notion of the perfectibility of man to be an illusion and argued that equality was unnatural because he believed that property and rank were fundamental to a Christian kingdom. He said that the revolutionaries had lurched back into savagery, undoing centuries of progress and development of civilization. His thinking was underpinned by fear of the mob. He lamented the destruction of the *ancien régime* and said that now 'the age of chivalry is gone ... the glory of Europe is extinguished forever'. By contrast, he argued for social *evolution* rather than revolution and stressed the continuity of history. Burke played an influential role in the development of the modern Conservative party in the nineteenth century and his writing underpinned the conservative strain in Romanticism which gained ground at that time.

Thomas Paine: *The Rights of Man Part I* (1791)

Paine was a republican who refuted Burke's ideas. An Enlightenment thinker, he vigorously asserted the power of reason and common sense to counter the injustice and privilege perpetrated by aristocracy and monarchy. He argued that such hierarchical social organization was in itself fraudulent, as men were created equal. Like Blake, who was a close friend, Paine wished to emphasize the real miseries suffered by ordinary people in the social structure defended by Burke. He was alerted by Blake to the government's intention to prosecute him for this publication and he fled to France. In his absence he was found guilty of treason and condemned, if he ever returned to England, to be hanged, drawn and quartered. Initially, he was warmly received in France but as a moderate was eventually imprisoned by the Jacobins and narrowly avoided the guillotine. He then fled to America, where his earlier writings had influenced the American revolutionaries alongside whom he had fought.

Philosophy

The most important figures here are Jean-Jacques Rousseau (1712–78) and William Godwin (1756-1836).

Jean-Jacques Rousseau: *Discourses* (1750, 1754); *The Social Contract* (1762)
Rousseau believed that feelings were more important than reason in human affairs. Unlike the philosopher Thomas Hobbes, who believed that human beings were naturally wicked, Rousseau argued that they were naturally good. He claimed that civilization, with its emphasis on property and power, corrupted human beings, in contrast to earlier philosophers who had claimed the *civilizing* influence of society. Rousseau promoted the idea of the Noble Savage. He stressed the importance of nature, which fostered natural instincts, as opposed to book-learning. Once separated from nature, human beings cease to be happy or virtuous. His view of the state of man in society is summed up in the famous sentence: 'Man is born free; and everywhere he is in chains' (*The Social Contract*). Rousseau did not deny the need for government, but said that it should always reflect the will of the people – a position endorsed by the American Declaration of Independence. He opposed tyrannical government and called for justice for the underprivileged. Rousseau's emphasis on freedom, the self, feelings, nature, and the primacy of childhood clearly had an enormous influence on the Romantic and revolutionary movements. However, Blake attacked him as an irreligious freethinker.

William Godwin: *An Enquiry concerning Political Justice* (1793)
In fact, Rousseau *did* influence Blake, through Blake's close friend William Godwin, who was himself a follower of Rousseau. Godwin was a radical and idealist with an almost impossibly high conception of the nobility of human beings and a total Enlightenment faith in reason. He attacked monarchy, aristocracy and social inequities of all kinds. Godwin believed that the rational human being was necessarily also benevolent and a lover of justice. The evil in the world, he thought, derived from property which promoted exploitation and inequality. Therefore the abolition of property, together with law, government, institutions and even marriage, would lead to human and social perfection. But Godwin could not support revolutionary action to achieve these ends as this would have involved the overthrow of reason. This explains why radicals as well as conservatives criticized his text. Godwin had a considerable impact on all the Romantic poets (especially Shelley). He also wrote a powerful novel, *Caleb Williams* (1794), which was both a vehicle for his ideas and an indictment of social oppression.

Religion

John Wesley (1703–91) was the founder of Methodism, an evangelical movement within the Church of England, which became a separate body in 1795. Wesley's ministry began about 1740 and was notable for his prodigious energy. During his lifetime he preached some 40,000 sermons, many delivered in the open air. Methodism stressed feeling as a route to God, and it is here that it made its contribution to the emergent Romantic movement, by contrast with the Augustans, for whom reason was the way to God: 'God said, *Let Newton be!* and all was light' (Pope). The singing of hymns (many of them written of course by Wesley himself) by the whole congregation was a new practice and helped characterize the fervent Methodist spirit. It seems likely that the vigorous, uplifting rhythms of Wesley's hymns are echoed in some of Blake's poems. Wesley particularly attracted the working class but Methodism spoke also to many middle-class people who felt excluded from the Established Church.

A footnote: utilitarianism and *laissez-faire* economics

In making their assault on the old hegemony of aristocracy and Established Church, the commercial and professional middle classes enlisted powerful new theories devised by their intellectual allies in the light of the emerging social and economic conditions. These theories too were the product of Enlightenment thinking and were to help shape the ideologies of the emerging urban, industrial Britain. The Romantics reacted against these theories and their social consequences. This is especially true of Blake, for whom industrialism and its theories were the fruits of Newtonian materialism, and served only to augment the suffering of ordinary people.

Jeremy Bentham (1748–1832) is the father-figure of utilitarianism. Bentham, a lawyer, set out to rationalize society's business arrangements. Starting from the assumption that human beings are fundamentally selfish, he proposed the idea of 'the greatest happiness of the greatest number' as a touchstone for social policy. He argued that less law meant more liberty, and that if the state left people alone, they would, by the pursuit of their own interests, automatically promote the greatest happiness of the greatest number. Initially, then, the theory was strongly non-interventionist but in the long run it led to far-reaching legal, social, political and economic reform later in the nineteenth century. In the period when Blake was writing, it was the source of much hardship and resentment.

The darker side to this theory is perhaps confirmed by the ideas of Thomas Malthus (1766–1834). His *Essay on the Principles of Population (as it affects the future improvement of society)* (1798) provided justification for a non-interventionist utilitarianism. He declared that population growth always outstrips the means of subsistence, therefore governments should let poverty – and the disease and starvation which inevitably follows from it – take its natural course to reduce numbers in society.

Utilitarians embraced wholesale the economic theories of Adam Smith (1723–90). His *The Wealth of Nations* (1776) endorsed free trade and competition in the market-place and revolutionized the economic theories of the day.

CRITICAL APPROACHES

Explorations and Activities

Blake as a visionary poet

In order to start to come to terms with Blake's poetry it is important first of all to understand Blake's characteristic 'ways of seeing'. Blake's visionary perspective which transforms reality may be unusual but this does not mean that he fails to see the material world accurately and clearly. This is especially true when he is describing social abuses.

'Twas on a Holy Thursday, their innocent faces clean,
The children walking two and two in red and blue and green,
Grey-headed beadles walked before, with wands as white as snow,
Till into the high dome of Paul's they like Thames' waters flow.
(*Holy Thursday*, **Songs of Innocence**)

In this example, Blake's description is more than documentary. His own capacity for imaginative insight was superior to the scientific perspective which relied on the eye to see and the reason to weigh and measure the physical world. Blake blamed this limited way of seeing on Newton:

... May God us keep
From single vision and Newton's sleep!
(*Letter in the form of a poem, to Thomas Butts*, 22 November 1802)

Elsewhere in the same poem Blake claims that there are even more complex ways of seeing:

Now I a fourfold vision see,
And a fourfold vision is given to me;
'Tis fourfold in my supreme delight
And threefold in soft Beulah's night
And twofold always.

Here Blake describes different levels of imaginative perception. While we must always reject the single vision of the scientists and cultivate a twofold vision, there are other levels of perception which enable us to envisage an earthly paradise (Beulah) – the threefold vision which comes to us in dreams – and, best of all, the fourfold vision which vouchsafes a glimpse of the supreme unity of heaven.

In *The Marriage of Heaven and Hell*, for example, the threefold vision creates a union of rationality and imagination (i.e. heaven and hell). The result is that we get a glimpse of an earthly paradise, in this case the liberation of humanity from the tyranny of Church and State. Crucially, Blake believed it was insufficient to rely on the eye to see the world, as the scientists and materialists did. The eye was a useful tool but insufficient unless working in combination with the creative imagination, which could transform mere sensory impressions and conjure up the visionary levels.

The fourfold vision is the supreme insight which reconciles all of the other levels and offers an almost mystical insight into the nature of the cosmos. The point is made in the wonderful lines which open the poem entitled *Auguries of Innocence*. The imagination, says Blake, can help us

To see a world in a grain of sand
And a heaven in a wild flower,
Hold infinity in the palm of your hand
And eternity in an hour.

In *Songs of Innocence* there is a repeated pattern in which the poet's perception first sees then transforms the material world (twofold vision), then projects an earthly paradise watched over by a loving God (threefold vision) while conceiving the whole in terms of a mystical joy immanent throughout the universe (fourfold vision). An understanding of this, of course, also helps us by contrast to come to terms with the evils and corruptions of the fallen, rationalist and materialist world described in *Songs of Experience*.

1 It is easier to find examples of different visionary dimensions in *Songs of Innocence*. Look again at *The Echoing Green, The Lamb, Laughing Song, A Cradle Song, Night*, and *A Dream*. Examine the ways in which Blake evokes: (i) the particular scene; (ii) an ideal world; (iii) a harmonious universe.

2 Now look at *The Little Girl Lost* and *The Little Girl Found* and *The Tiger*, for example, in *Songs of Experience*. You will find these more challenging poems, but they too reveal the same processes at work.

Blake's use of symbolism

A characteristic feature of Blake's imaginative vision is his ability to 'think' in symbols and images. Because of this, at first glance it might appear that he is out of touch with everyday life but this would not be true – and indeed he has a lively awareness of the social and political realities of his time. As a child, Blake had vivid dreams and nightmares which evolved into a way of seeing which depended on a complex system of symbols, and it was through this that he expressed his radical philosophy of life. He dramatized his ideas by drawing on this symbol system. Properly speaking, this is what we mean when we describe Blake as a visionary.

Blake's personal symbol system was derived from many sources, including his childhood dreams and nightmares, and from his reading in literature, politics and philosophy. Central to successful ways of reading Blake to is to be alert to the novel way in which he employed some familiar symbols and images. You cannot take it for granted in Blake's poems that the symbol means what you expect it to mean. This is one of the ways in which Blake challenged the conventional values of his time. For example in *The Marriage of Heaven and Hell*, 'heaven' stands for rationalism, materialism, lack of faith, lack of true humility, repression; 'hell' on the other hand, stands for imagination, energy, engagement, freedom, true spirituality. He even depicts Satan as an heroic, revolutionary figure.

London from ***Songs of Experience*** is an important poem which highlights the complexity of Blake's symbolism. As in other poems, a reader needs to be aware of levels of meaning and the application of new, sometimes quite shocking, meanings to familiar symbols. The title announces that this is going to be a poem about London, which at the end of the eighteenth century was becoming a great financial and commercial centre of world significance. 'London', however, becomes a symbol not only of the city itself, but also of the state of English society and the human condition. By the end of the poem, Blake has completely revised any complacent ideas a reader might have about London as a centre of civilization.

London

I wander through each chartered street
Near where the chartered Thames does flow,
And mark in every face I meet
Marks of weakness, marks of woe.

In every cry of every man,
In every infant's cry of fear,
In every voice, in every ban,
The mind-forged manacles I hear.

How the chimney-sweeper's cry
Every black'ning church appals,
And the hapless soldier's sigh
Runs in blood down palace walls.

But most through midnight streets I hear
How the youthful harlot's curse
Blasts the newborn infant's tear,
And blights with plagues the marriage hearse.

By careful use of symbolism, the poem develops from specific observations into a disturbing vision of a society in crisis. Blake achieves this partly through repetition of words which take on new levels of symbolic meaning each time they appear.

For example, the first reference to 'chartered' sounds innocuous enough and may indeed suggest something worthy – commercial enterprise, the rights of citizens and so on. But when it is repeated, in the second line, as a description of the Thames the reader becomes aware of other possible meanings which are much less positive. When applied to a flowing river, 'chartered' may simply mean mapping its course, but could also imply restraint and constriction, the inhibition of natural vitality. This then leads the reader to wonder whether Blake is talking about the state of mind of the inhabitants, whom we meet in the very next line.

1   There are other repetitions, e.g. 'mark(s)', 'cry'. Consider the effect of these and how different levels of meaning are generated.

The poem seems to hinge on the central symbol of the 'mind-forged manacles'. In this very powerful symbol, Blake at once explains the sufferings of the people (their cries and marks) and begins to open up the causes of their oppression. And while the physical suffering is real, Blake suggests that the more profound source of the problem lies in attitudes of mind which are inimical to freedom of thought and imagination. The manacles signify a prison of contemporary ideologies located in the Church and State which Blake now goes on to illuminate.

2 Closely examine the vision of the final two stanzas and consider how Blake exploits the symbolism in order to show how and why London has become the inversion of a desirable human society and is approaching catastrophe.

Whenever you read a poem by Blake you have to explore the symbolism. Some poems will give up their meanings more easily than others, but some remain elusive and this is part of their power. Their elusive nature depends crucially on their use of symbolism.

3 Look again at *The Blossom* and *Infant Joy* from **Songs of Innocence** and *The Sick Rose* and *The Tiger* from **Songs of Experience**, and closely examine the symbols Blake employs. How does the symbolism extend the possible layers of meaning in the poems?

Blake's dialectics

In addition to the symbols themselves, Blake devised particular notions of the nature of symbolic thinking or ways of thinking in symbols. Blake saw human experience as a constant battle between two forces which he called the Spectre and the Emanation. The Spectre was all of those things that Blake hated and which he saw as active in late eighteenth-century life: centrally, the tyranny of the intellect, reason and mechanistic thinking, all of which gave rise to political oppression and repressive religion. The Emanation, on the other hand, arose from that which Blake saw as positive: the God-like power of the imagination, instinct and freedom – all those things that enable human beings to fulfil their potential. These were the qualities that Blake hoped would be released by the American and French Revolutions and which he promoted in his own writings.

Blake's way of seeing is contingent upon his recognition of the continuing struggle between these opposing forces. This is what we understand by Blake's dialectics: an idea can only be defined by the existence of its opposite Thus the dialectical thinker has a love of paradox, rejects categorization, and accepts the inevitability of conflict and change. New perceptions arise from the series of conflicts that arise when opposing ideas clash. The difference between Blake and what he saw as the oppressors in late eighteenth-century England was that he welcomed difference, whereas the Church and the State sought to suppress it.

This is clearly illustrated in *The Marriage of Heaven and Hell* where Blake introduces the doctrine of contraries:

Without contraries is no progression. Attraction and repulsion, reason and energy, love and hate, are necessary to human existence.

From these contraries spring what the religious call good and evil. Good is the passive that obeys reason, evil is the active springing from energy.

Good is heaven; evil is hell. (*Plate 3*)

1 From your own experience, consider the ways in which contraries can result in progression.

2 To what extent would you concur with the idea that 'Attraction and repulsion, reason and energy, love and hate' are necessary to human existence?

Blake believed that the French Revolution marked the beginning of a new era: a new heaven on earth, a heaven of liberty and equality. This had been initiated, however, by the 'hell' of the revolutionary energies released. The old order of State and Church would certainly view these events as 'hell'. Paradoxically, Blake's vision sees these 'infernal' energies as creating a true 'heaven', i.e. the marriage of heaven and hell.

In *Songs of Innocence and of Experience* Blake goes on to give poetic expression to some of these more abstract ideas. In the light of the above, you should be developing an understanding of Blake's motives in pairing collections of poems of 'Innocence' and 'Experience'. Blake wants to heighten the reader's awareness of the two 'contrary states of the human soul' by playing them off against each other. His dialectical habit of mind is not only evident across the collections, but also within individual poems in each collection. There are some obviously paired poems which examine the contrary states. Equally, many of the individual poems in each collection show an awareness of the contrary state, i.e. some poems in *Songs of Innocence* hint at the perils of experience, while some poems in *Songs of Experience* resonate with a sense of the absence of innocence, a sense of loss.

3 Read the following paired poems and consider the ways in which Blake manages to enhance an understanding of the contrary states:

The Lamb	*The Tiger*
The Chimney Sweeper	*The Chimney Sweeper*
Holy Thursday	*Holy Thursday*
Nurse's Song	*Nurse's Song*
Infant Joy	*Infant Sorrow*

4 Read *The Echoing Green* and *On Another's Sorrow* from **Songs of Innocence** and *The Garden of Love* and *A Little Girl Lost* from **Songs of Experience**. Consider the way in which the contrary state is hinted at in these poems and how this contributes to the total effect.

Themes in Blake's poetry

There are certain characteristic themes in Blake's poetry and although they often overlap, they are worth separate consideration, if only to bring them into focus. These are some of the more specific ways in which Blake pursues the dialectic of innocence and experience. They emerge both as part of Blake's indignation at conditions in late eighteenth-century England and as part of his healing visions. They are, of course, delivered explicitly and implicitly in his patterns of symbolism. An exploration of the following key themes will deepen an understanding of the poems and Blake's relationship to contemporary conditions.

Innocence

1 What means (tone, language, symbols) does Blake employ in order to establish the world of innocence in **Songs of Innocence**? Look at *Introduction, The Shepherd, Laughing Song* and *Spring*.

Blake's understanding of innocence was not grounded in an absence of understanding, rather, it was a consequence of insight into the mysteries of the cosmos. In other words we should not underestimate the complexity of Blake's understanding of innocence. He was never sentimental or naïve about innocence. He once wrote:

Unorganized innocence: an impossibility. Innocence dwells with wisdom, but never with ignorance.

> (Note written on the back of an edition of **The Four Zoas**)

As with much of Blake's writing, the reader should be alert to levels of meaning, in this case, from simple child-like innocence to a vision of a universe of love and harmony.

2 Contrast the representation of innocence in the poems mentioned in the previous activity with *The Cradle Song* and *The Divine Image*.

Guardians

In Blake, innocence is not entirely the preserve of children; it is also manifested in the attitude and actions of men and women filled with the spirit of the divine as in the two poems considered above. A central theme in Blake's poetry is that of guardianship. The successful guardian is the adult who listens, who is alert to the voice of innocence and responds appropriately.

3 Read *The Shepherd*, *The Echoing Green* and *Nurse's Song* (from **Songs of Innocence**). Consider the role of the adult in each case.

4 Contrast these with poems where adults impose their values on children. Read *Infant Sorrow* and *Nurse's Song* (**Songs of Experience**)

5 Read *The Little Boy Lost* and *The Little Boy Found* (**Songs of Experience**). How do these poems extend Blake's exploration of the theme of guardianship?

Social and political themes

Blake's sympathy for the suffering of ordinary men, women and children in the real world was profound. He was a friend and associate of many radicals of the time including Thomas Paine. He may be seen as a visionary but he was also acutely aware of social and political realities, as we have seen in the discussion of *London*, and was particularly appalled by the complacency of the Church in respect of social abuse.

It is in this theme that some of the others coalesce. An extension of his interest in innocence is a concern for the vulnerable and exploited, especially children. Conversely he targets those adults who represent the worst features of the failure of guardianship.

6 *The Chimney Sweeper* and *Holy Thursday* (in both **Songs of Innocence** and **Songs of Experience**) describe exploitation by corrupt adults. How is Blake's indignation at the social abuses described in these poems communicated? How successfully in each case does innocence resist oppression?

7 Read *The Schoolboy*, which takes up the theme of the vulnerability of innocence. In what way is it different from the previous group of poems? Is the net effect the same?

Blake was a fervent supporter of the French Revolution, which he believed would eradicate tyrannical monarchs and false religion. He articulates much of this in *The Marriage of Heaven and Hell*. *The Tiger* is a complex poem which has been interpreted in a number of ways: one of these is as a celebration of revolutionary energies that cleanse a corrupt world and establish a new order.

8 Read Plates 2 and 3 and *A Song of Liberty* (Plates 25-27) from *The Marriage of Heaven and Hell,* and *The Tiger.* How successful is Blake in representing his social and political thinking in these works? How does this examination contribute to your understanding of *The Tiger*?

Conventional religion

Blake was particularly hostile towards conventional religion and especially the Church of England which he included amongst the 'dark satanic mills' in *And did those feet in ancient time*.

The Enlightenment rationalism that arose from Newton's physics also shaped forms of belief in eighteenth-century England. Blake attacked the priesthood of the Church of England for promoting a rational religion which denied the divinity in the human. In *The Marriage of Heaven and Hell*, Blake argues that a faith based on reason is a denial of desire (energy). A 'Thou shalt not' morality (see *The Garden of Love* in **Songs of Experience**) leads only to corruption and a passive response to authority: 'Good is the passive that obeys reason' (Plate 3). The rational (i.e. repressive) Church is instrumental in the process of closing up the 'doors of perception' (Plate 14) and deprives human beings of sight of the infinite.

9 Blake concludes *The Marriage of Heaven and Hell* with the following:
>Let the priests of the raven of dawn no longer, in deadly black, with hoarse note, curse the sons of joy; nor his accepted brethren (whom, tyrant, he calls free) lay the bound or build the roof; nor pale religious lechery call that virginity that wishes but acts not.
>For everything that lives is holy.

In your own words, summarize Blake's attitude towards the Church and the clergy. Find two or three other occasions when Blake attacks them in similar terms.

Blake's attack on the false guardians took on particular significance when he turned his attention to the clergy, whom he described as corrupt, parasitical and repressive (see, for example 'the villain' and 'the sneaking serpent' in *The Marriage of Heaven and Hell* (Plate 2).

10 Read *The Garden of Love, The Little Vagabond* and *A Little Boy Lost* from **Songs of Experience**. How does Blake's exploitation of symbolism further his attack on the clergy? What is Blake's ideal 'contrary state' to the image of religion and priesthood offered in these poems?

11 Read *The Human Abstract* and *And did those feet in ancient time*. Trace Blake's understanding of the processes by which evil and corruption came into human society and how they will be eradicated.

Love and sexuality

What is notable about Blake in the religious and moral climate of the times is his celebration of sexuality because of its association with innocence, energy and desire. Look again at *A Little Girl Lost* in **Songs of Experience**. As this shows, he was also aware of the potential of sexuality to be corrupted in a world of experience. This dialectical opposition is revealed in the symbolism of *The Blossom* and its contrary *The Sick Rose*.

12 In a short sequence of poems in **Songs of Experience**, Blake reflects on both the potential of human sexuality and the hazards it faces in the world of experience. Read *My Pretty Rose-Tree*, *Ah, Sunflower!*, *The Lily* and *The Garden of Love* and consider in detail the conclusions that Blake reaches, and the symbolic means he employs.

On being an artist

Blake firmly believed that his art would make a contribution to the moral, spiritual and intellectual revolution he envisaged. In this respect he was in line with other conceptions of the Romantic artist – the inspired genius with special insight and visionary powers. Artists were distinguished by the powers of their creative imagination.

13 In *The Marriage of Heaven and Hell* Blake conveys his own artistic manifesto and his wish to dedicate his prophetic craft to achieve social renewal. Refer again to Plates 6–7, 12–13, 14 and 23–24 and summarize Blake's understanding of the importance and role of the poet.

14 How would you account for the transition from piper (*Introduction* in **Songs of Innocence**) to bard (*Introduction*, *Earth's Answer* and *The Voice of the Ancient Bard* in **Songs of Experience**)? Examine closely the bard's message, tone and rhetorical style. Is there a further change in the final poem?

ESSAYS

1 William Blake has been described as the only English prophet. With close reference to two or three poems in *Songs of Innocence and of Experience*, discuss the validity of this claim.

2 Compare *The Lamb* with *The Tiger*. How successfully does Blake explore the 'contrary states of the human soul' in these two poems?

3 'Blake hated tyranny and celebrated liberty but he did not reject leadership altogether – the crucial thing for him was the nature of that leadership.' With close reference to two or three poems from *Songs of Innocence and of Experience*, explore Blake's conception of wise guardianship.

4 'For Blake the imagination is nothing less than God as He operates in the human soul.' (C. M. Bowra) Briefly summarize Blake's understanding of the powers of the creative imagination with reference to *The Marriage of Heaven and Hell* and select for analysis one or two poems from *Songs of Innocence and of Experience* where he exemplifies this idea.

5 *The Marriage of Heaven and Hell* can be thought of as Blake's intellectual and artistic manifesto. Select one of the following themes found in this text and show how it is given poetic treatment in one (or two) poems in *Songs of Innocence and of Experience*:

the role of the poet

the attack on the Established Church

political oppression

What is gained from the poetic treatment of the theme?

6 Choose two poems from *Songs of Innocence* and two poems from *Songs of Experience* that have appealed to you in some way. Comment on Blake's use of language in each case and the way in which this has contributed to your understanding of the theme(s) explored. Why do these poems interest you?

7 'For Blake, human sexuality was an ambivalent entity, capable of generating the joy of innocence but also plunging the individual into the misery of experience.' Examine the complex treatment of this theme by selecting at least two poems from both *Songs of Innocence* and *Songs of Experience*.

8 'For personal and political reasons, Blake's mood had darkened between the writing of *Songs of Innocence* and *Songs of Experience*.' What would you identify as the main differences between the representation of the human condition in each series of poems? Refer to at least two poems from each series in your answer.

9 Blake hated the 'centralised tyranny of the intellect'. Show how he communicates his indignation with reference to two or three poems in *Songs of Innocence and of Experience*.

10 'It is a characteristic of the Romantic poet to envisage an ideal world with which to compare the real world: it is in part that idealism which hopes for social revolution.' With reference to a selection of poems in *Songs of Innocence and of Experience*, describe the elements of Blake's 'ideal world'.

11 'Natural objects always did and do now weaken, deaden and obliterate imagination in me.' (William Blake) Unlike the later Romantics (e.g. Wordsworth), Blake is never thought of as a nature poet and always gave primacy to the human imagination. However, with reference to a selection of poems in *Songs of Innocence*, show how Blake could nevertheless celebrate the natural world.

12 Blake lived at a time when the English landscape was undergoing dramatic changes – principally because of the growth of towns and urbanization. With reference to *Songs of Experience*, *And did those feet in ancient time* and *Auguries of Innocence*, show how even this most visionary of poets was also sharply aware of the realities of city life.

13 Discuss Blake's treatment of specific social abuses of his time by selecting paired poems from *Songs of Innocence and of Experience*. How does the approach differ in each series?

WRITING AN ESSAY
ABOUT POETRY

Your own personal response to a poet and his or her work is of major importance when writing an essay on poetry, either as part of your course or as an examination question. However, this personal response needs to be based on a solid concept of how poetry works, so you must clearly show that you understand the methods the poet uses to convey the message and ideas of the poem to the reader. In most cases, unless it is relevant to your answer, you should not pad out your essay with biographical or background material.

Planning

Look carefully at the wording of the question. Underline the important words and ideas. Make sure you apply your mind to these key elements of the question and then explore them in the essay.

Bring all your knowledge of, and opinions on, a poet and his or her poetry to this first stage of writing. Brainstorm your ideas and always combine these thoughts in a plan that shows the development and intention of your answer. Your plan must outline the structure of your essay. In exam conditions, the plan and the direction of your comments may take you only a few minutes and should be little more than a way of laying out your ideas in order. However the plan must be an outline of how and where you are going to link your evidence to the opinions and concepts of the essay. Reject any ideas which are not relevant at the planning stage. Remember that your plan should be arranged around your ideas and not the chronological order of a poem or a poet's work, or your essay will be weakened.

Writing

Your introduction must implicitly or, if you wish, explicitly make the teacher or examiner realize that you understand the question.

Don't spend a lot of time spotting, defining and examining poetic techniques and form. If you do identify these features, then you must be sure of the poetic terms and be able to show why they are significant in the verse and to the poet's attempts to create a 'meaning' and a message.

Make absolutely sure that your answer is clear and that it tackles the issues in the question precisely. Try to offer points for discussion and apply your knowledge in an interesting way. Don't go ahead and disregard what the question asks you to write about, then write the essay you want to write. Don't waffle, don't write too elaborately or use terms vaguely; at the same time, don't be too heavy-handed with your views. Strive to put your opinions directly and accurately.

In exam conditions be aware of the time, and if you are running out of your allotted span then make sure that you put down your most important ideas in the minutes left. Try to leave a few minutes to revise and proof-read your script. Be sure that the points you have made make sense and are well supported by evidence. Don't try to introduce new ideas as you write unless they are essential to your essay. Often these extra thoughts can distract you from the logic of your argument. If it is essential, then refer back to your plan and slot the idea into the right part of the essay.

Bring your ideas together at the end of the essay. Make sure that you have put your views clearly and, if necessary, express the main thrust of your views or argument again.

Quotations

Quotations are a vital source of evidence for the viewpoints and ideas you express in your essay. Try not to misquote and remember that when using extracts of more than a few words you should place them separately outside your text as they would be laid out in the poem.

If you follow the advice here you will produce a clear, relevant and logical essay. Try to spend time reading and listening to the comments of your teacher and make your own notes on your work for revision purposes.

A NOTE FROM A CHIEF EXAMINER

Your examination script is the medium through which you communicate with your examiner. As a student, you will have studied what writers say and how they say it; your examiner will assess what *you* say and how you say it. This is the simple process through which your knowledge and understanding of the texts you have studied is converted into your examination result.

The questions which you will find on your examination paper have been designed to enable you to display your ability to engage in short, highly concentrated explorations of particular aspects of the texts which you have studied. There is no intention to trick you into making mistakes, rather to enable you to demonstrate to your examiner your knowledge and understanding. Questions take a variety of forms. For a poetry text, you may be asked to concentrate on one poem, or a particular group of them, and provide detailed examination of some features of the writing. You may be asked to range widely throughout a poet's work, exploring specified aspects of his or her style and themes. You may be asked to provide a considered personal reaction to a critical evaluation of the poet's work.

Whatever the question, you are, ultimately, being asked to explore what and how, content and style. Equally, you are being asked for a personal response. You are communicating to your examiner your own understanding of the text, and your reactions to it, based on the studies you have undertaken.

All of this may seem very simple, if not self-evident, but it is worthwhile to devote some time to thinking about what an examination is, and how it works. By doing so, you will understand why it is so important that you should prepare yourself for your examination in two principal ways: first, by thorough, thoughtful and analytical textual study, making your own well-informed evaluation of the work of a particular writer, considering what he or she is conveying to you, how this is done, how you react, and what has made you respond in that way; then, by practising the writing skills which you will need to convey all these things to your examiner.

When assessing your script and awarding marks, examiners are working to guidelines which instruct them to look for a variety of different qualities in an essay.

These are some of the things which an examiner will consider.

- How well has the candidate understood the essay question and the given task? Is the argument, and the material used to support it, entirely relevant?

- Is quotation used aptly, and textual reference employed skilfully in discussion?

- Is the candidate aware of how and why the writer has crafted material in a particular way?

- Is there evidence of engagement with the text, close analytical reading, and awareness of subtleties in interpretation?

- Does the candidate have the necessary vocabulary, both general and critical, to express his or her understanding lucidly? Are technical terms integrated into discussion?

- Can the candidate provide an interesting, clearly expressed and structured line of argument, which fully displays a well-informed personal response?

From these points, you should be able to see the kind of approach to examination questions which you should avoid. Re-hashed notes, second-hand opinion, unsupported assertion and arid copies of marginal jottings have no place in a good script. Don't fall into the trap of reproducing a pre-planned essay. Undoubtedly you will find (if your preparation has been thorough) that you are drawing on ideas which you have already explored in other essays, but all material used must be properly adapted to the task you are given. Don't take a narrative approach; paraphrase cannot replace analysis. Do not, under any circumstances, copy out chunks of introduction or critical notes from your text in an open book examination. Nor do you need to quote at excessive length; your examiner knows the text.

It is inevitable that, when writing in examination conditions, you will only use quite a small amount of the material you have studied in order to answer a particular question. Don't feel that what you are not using has been wasted. It hasn't. All your studies will have informed the understanding you display in a succinct, well-focused answer, and will equip you to write a good essay.

Virginia Graham

SELECT BIBLIOGRAPHY

Editions

Keynes, G. (ed.) (1970): *Blake: Songs of Innocence and of Experience*. Oxford: Oxford University Press.

Available in paperback, this edition reproduces in the original size and colours Blake's plates for **Songs of Innocence and of Experience**, showing the poems and accompanying designs exactly as they would have appeared to the original readers. Keynes' introduction and commentaries on the poems are also useful.

Keynes, G. (ed.) (1975): *The Marriage of Heaven and Hell*. Oxford: Oxford University Press.

This is the companion volume to the one described above and follows the same format.

Mason, M. (ed.) (1988): *William Blake*. Oxford: Oxford University Press.

This is a useful edition if you wish to extend your reading of Blake beyond the poems included in the present volume.

Biography

Ackroyd, P. (1995): *Blake*. London: Sinclair Stevenson.

This new biography has been described as a masterpiece and could well become the definitive life of Blake. It contains helpful readings of the poems and in particular a brilliant account of the composition, and symbolism, of *The Tiger*.

Wilson, M. (1971): *The Life of William Blake*. Oxford: Oxford University Press.

This is an accessible and readable biography.

Further reading

Bloom, H. (1991): *Blake*. New York: Chelsea House Publishers.

This is a stimulating, if sometimes challenging, collection of recent essays on Blake's writings which reflects the renewed interest in Blake and the other Romantic poets among modern literary scholars.

Bottrall, M. (ed.) (1970): *William Blake: Songs of Innocence and of Experience, A Selection of Critical Essays*. London: Macmillan.

Although perhaps a little dated now, this collection of essays nevertheless contains some illuminating readings of particular poems. A new casebook, containing recent critical readings, is promised in 1996.

Butler, M. (1981): *Romantics, Rebels and Reactionaries*. Oxford: Oxford University Press.

This is a key text in modern studies of the Romantic poets and provides excellent contextual material.

Ferber, M. (1991): *The Poetry of William Blake*. Harmondsworth: Penguin Books.

This is especially helpful for new readers of Blake. Ferber lucidly resolves textual difficulties and treats all the works, including the Prophetic Books, chronologically. The poems are discussed in conjunction with the illustrations which accompanied them.

Ferber, M. (1985): *The Social Vision of William Blake*. Princeton, N.J.: Princeton University Press.

This is a demanding but rewarding book which sets Blake's thought in its intellectual and social context.

Ford, B.(ed.) (1982): *From Blake to Byron: New Pelican Guide to English Literature* Volume 5. Harmondsworth: Penguin Books.

This contains an introductory essay on Blake for new readers.

Gardner, S. (1986): *Blake's Innocence and Experience Retraced*. London: The Athlone Press.

A useful re-reading of the poems and in particular the nature of the 'two contrary states'. Gardner also looks at the relationship between the poems and the illustrations, and draws on Blake's life and times where this aids understanding.

Glen, H. (1983): *Vision and Disenchantment: Blake's Songs and Wordsworth's Lyrical Ballads*. Cambridge: Cambridge University Press.

This is a very interesting reading of both collections and is especially good on the innovative nature of **Songs of Innocence and of Experience**.

Larrissy, E. (1985): *William Blake*. Oxford: Blackwell.

Larrissy discusses Blake's contradictory attitudes towards Enlightenment thinking, i.e. admiration for its advocacy of liberty, democracy and the rights of man but hatred of its rationalism.

Lindsay, D. (1989): *Songs of Innocence and of Experience*. London: The Critics Debate Series.

The aim of this series is to review the range of criticism devoted to particular works. In this case, it provides an invaluable sense of the variety of readings – and critical disputes – which **Songs of Innocence and of Experience** have attracted.

Prickett, S. (ed.) (1981): *The Romantics*. London: Methuen.

As the series title suggests, this text provides useful contextual reading for a study of the Romantic movement in Britain by reviewing contemporary social and historical events as well as developments in art, religion, philosophy and politics.

Thompson E.P. (1993): *Witness Against the Beast: William Blake and the Moral Law*. Cambridge: Cambridge University Press.

This provides a readable and very thought-provoking historical context against which Blake's work can be set. It includes a chapter on *London*.

Watson, J. R. (1992): *English Poetry of the Romantic Period 1789-1830*. London: Longman.

This is an impressive survey of Romanticism and the Romantic poets and contains an excellent chapter on Blake.

INDEX OF FIRST LINES